The White CHristmas

And Other

Merry Christmas Plays

WALTER BEN HARE

[ZHINGOORA BOOKS]

This edition is published by
Zhingoora Books.

The Cover is Designed by Pallav Sethiya.

zhingoora_books@yahoo.com

CONTENTS

THE WHITE CHRISTMAS

JOSEPH · MARY · SIMEON · TIMOTHY · ISAAC · ANNA · THOMAS · RUTH · RACHEL · DEBORAH · PRISCILLA · MELCHIOR · GASPAR · BALTASAR · PROLOGUE

THE WHITE CHRISTMAS

A CHRISTMAS MORALITY PLAY IN ONE ACT.

Originally produced by the Quadrangle Club of the University of Missouri, Christmas Eve, 1909.

CHARACTERS.

Mary	*The Maiden Mother*
Joseph	*Of the House of David*
Simeon	*An Old Shepherd*
Timothy	*A Shepherd, the Husband of Anna*
Isaac	*A Young Shepherd*
Anna	*The Wife of Timothy, the Shepherd*
Thomas	*Her Little Son*
Ruth	*Her Little Daughter*
Deborah	*Hostess of an Inn at Bethlehem*
Rachel	*A Maiden of Bethlehem*
Priscilla	*Her Cousin*

Melchoir }
Gaspar   } *The Wise Men from the East.*
Baltasar }

A Concealed Choir. The Prologue.

For description of costumes, arrangement of the scene, etc., see "Remarks on the Production" at the end of the play.

Time of Playing—*About One Hour.*

Scene I: *Before the play begins the* Prologue *steps in front of the curtains and addresses the congregation.*

Prologue.

The earth has grown old with its burden of care,
But at Christmas it always is young,
The heart of the jewel burns lustrous and fair,
And its soul, full of music, bursts forth on the air,
When the song of the angels is sung.

It is coming, Old Earth, it is coming tonight!
On the snowflakes which cover thy sod
The feet of the Christ Child fall gentle and white,
And the voice of the Christ Child tells out with delight,
That mankind are the children of God.

On the sad and the lonely, the wretched and poor,
The voice of the Christ Child shall fall;
And to every blind wanderer open the door
Of hope that he dared not to dream of before,
With a sunshine of welcome for all.
—*Phillips Brooks.*

And it came to pass in those days, that there went out a decree from Cæsar Augustus, that all the world should be taxed. And this taxing was first made when Cyrenius was governor of Syria. And all went to be taxed, every one into his own city.

And Joseph also went up from Galilee, out of the city of Nazareth, into Judea, unto the city of David, which is called Bethlehem, because he was of the house and lineage of David. To be taxed with Mary his espoused wife....

And so it was, that, while they were there, the days were accomplished that she should be delivered. And she brought forth her first born son, and wrapped him in swaddling clothes, and laid him in a manger; because there was no room for them in the inn. (*Exit* Prologue.)

(*Soft chimes. As these chimes die away in the distance a concealed choir is heard singing.*)

O COME, COME, AWAY.

O come, come away
From labor now reposing,
Let busy care a while forbear;
O come, come away.

(The front curtains are drawn, showing a winter street in Bethlehem. No one appears on the stage, but the choir continues singing outside at right front.)

Come, come, our social joys renew,
And thus where trust and friendship grew,
Let true hearts welcome you,
O come, come away.

Rachel *and* Priscilla *enter from the inn at right front, arm in arm. They go to the center, then to the rear of the stage, turn and face the inn, pause a moment or two, listening to the choir, and then go out at rear left. The choir continues:*

From toils and the cares
On which the day is closing,
The hour of eve brings sweet reprieve,
O come, come away.
O come where love will smile on thee,
And round its hearth will gladness be,
And time fly merrily,
O come, come away.

While the choir is singing the last three lines of the song, Simeon *and* Isaac *enter from rear left, leaning on their shepherd's crooks. They pause at rear center and listen to the singing. When the song is finished the organ continues the same music softly.*

Simeon.
Make haste, my son, the hour is waxing late,
The night is cold, methinks our sheep await.

Isaac.
Nay gran'ther, I would liefer tarry here.
The town is gay, the inns are full of cheer.

Simeon (*points to rear right*).
But there our duty lies, the wind grows cold!
Come, let's away and put the sheep in fold.

(*Starts off right.*)

Isaac.
Nay, Simeon, wait! What means this crowd of men
And women here in peaceful Bethlehem?

Simeon (*comes to him*).
Herod the King hath issued a decree
That each and all his subjects taxèd be;
And every one who in this town saw light
Must here return and register tonight.
From all Judea, aye, from th' distant land,
Each Bethlehemite must come at his command.

Isaac (*comes to the doorway of the inn and peers in*).
The town is full of people, great and small,
Each inn is crowded to its very wall.

Simeon (*comes down center and takes his arm*).
But come, we're wasting time, 'tis very late.
Make haste, my son, I know the flocks await!

Isaac.

Thou speakest true, though I would rather stay,
Our duty calls, so to the hills, away!

(They go out at rear right.)

*The concealed choir repeats the first stanza of the song softly. After a slight
pause* Deborah *enters from the inn.*

Deborah (*coming down to right front*).
My inn is crowded to the doors. The heat
Is stifling, but out here the air is sweet.

(Looks upward.)

The bright stars twinkle with mysterious light,
Methinks there's something strange about the night.

She sits on the bench in front of the inn. Timothy *enters from rear
left.* Deborah *continues her soliloquy.*

The air is still, the night is very cold,
The shepherds seek the hills to watch the fold.

(Sees him.)

(Timothy *goes out at rear R.*)

Deborah.
Some strange, unearthly voice seems calling me,
Methinks this night portends great things to be.

Enter Rachel *and* Priscilla *from rear right, then come down center and
address the hostess.*

Rachel.
Hail, hostess of the inn, my cousin here
Hath lodgings at your inn. We'd seek its cheer.

Deborah (*rises*).
Enter within. My guests tonight are gay
And fain would turn this winter's night to day.

Rachel *and* Priscilla *enter the inn, followed by* Deborah. *The organ music continues softly. After a slight pause enter* Anna *from rear left. She leads* Ruth *and* Thomas *by the hand.*

Thomas (*at rear center*).
Oh, mother, hark! There's music in the inn!

Anna.
'Tis not for us—their noise and merry din.

Ruth.
Our little town is crowded, joyous, gay.

Thomas.
So many travelers came this way today.

Ruth.
The night is chill and cold, I much do fear
The little sheep will shiver by the mere.

Anna.
Too cold it is for thee, I fear, in truth,
Return and get thy cloak, my little Ruth.
We'll wait for thee upon the little hill.

(*Points off R.*)

But speed thy steps, the cold will work thee ill.

Ruth.
I'll fly, dear mother, like an arrow home.

(*Runs out at L.*)

Anna.
We must not tarry. Come, my Thomas, come!

(*She leads him out at rear R. There is a pause. The music changes to a mysterious plaintive air. The old German song, Holy Night, may be effectively introduced as an organ solo.*)

Enter from rear right, Joseph, *walking with a staff and supporting* Mary.

Mary.
Here is a place, now I must rest awhile!
For many a league, for many a weary mile,
We've trudged along since break of day began.

Joseph.
'Tis true, and I'm an old and ancient man,
My joints are stiff, my bones are waxing old—
And the long night is bitter, bitter cold.
Here take my cloak and keep thee warm within,
And wait thee here while I search out an inn.

(*He wraps his cloak around her and seats her on the bench or stool in front of the manger. He goes out at rear left. The music changes to the Magnificat, to be found in all Episcopal hymnals.*)

Mary (*sings*).
My soul doth magnify the Lord: and my spirit hath rejoiced in God my Saviour.
For he hath regarded: the lowliness of his handmaiden.
For behold, from henceforth: all generations shall call me blessed.
For he that is mighty has magnified me: and holy is his Name.
And his mercy is on them that fear him: throughout all generations.
He hath showed strength with his arm: he hath scattered the proud in the imagination of their hearts.

He hath put down the mighty from their seat: and hath exalted the humble and meek.

He hath filled the hungry with good things: and the rich he hath sent empty away.

He remembering his mercy hath holpen his servant Israel: as he promised to our forefathers, Abraham and his seed, forever.

Enter Joseph *from rear L.*

Joseph.
For hours I've trudged the street in fruitless quest,
Here is an inn, mayhap at last we'll rest.

Enter Deborah *from the inn.*

Mary.
Husband, I'm faint; I can no farther go.
Methinks I'll rest me here upon this loe.

(*Sits in front of the manger.*)

Joseph (*assisting her*).
Have courage, Mary, here's the hostess here.

(*Comes to* Deborah *at right.*)

We'd lodge with thee tonight.

Deborah.
Alas, I fear
My inn is crowded to the very wall,
Soldiers and scribes, the rich, the great, the small!

Joseph.
Is there room for us? My wife is ill.

Deborah.

My heart is sad and it is not my will
To send you hence, but naught is left to do.
Perhaps some other inn will shelter you.

Joseph.
Alas, the other inns are all the same!

Deborah.
Never was seen the like in Bethlehem.

(*Laughter and noise at R.*)

My guests are merry, hear their jovial din!

(*Goes to R.*)

I pity you, there's no room at the inn.

(*Exits into the inn.*)

Mary.
Our last hope gone! Now, what shall we do?
My strength is leaving!

(*Bows head.*)

Joseph.
Would I could succor you.
I'll wrap thee warm. Now rest thee here a while.
We've traveled far, full many a weary mile.

Enter Ruth *from rear L., hurrying along.*

Joseph.
Maiden, I fain would stop thee in thy flight—
Can'st tell where we could lodge this winter night?

Ruth.
That inn is crowded. There's one upon the hill.

Joseph.
I've tried them all, my wife is very ill.

Ruth.
That little stable there upon the loe,

(*Points to L front.*)

'Tis snug and warm. 'Twill shield thee from the snow.

Mary (*rises*).
God's blessing on thy little head, sweet child!
Come, Joseph, for the wind now waxes wild.

(*Exits L. front.*)

(Joseph *leads her to exit L., then turns and looks off R.*)

Joseph.

O little town of Bethlehem,
How still we see thee lie!
Above thy deep and dreamless sleep
The silent stars go by.
Yet in thy dark streets shineth
(*Turns toward manger.*)
The everlasting Light;
The hopes and fears of all the years
Are met in thee tonight.

(Ruth *stands at rear C., watching him.*)

The curtains slowly fall.

Scene II: *Hymn by the congregation.*

WHILE SHEPHERDS WATCHED THEIR FLOCKS.

While shepherds watched their flocks by night,
All seated on the ground.
The angel of the Lord came down,
And glory shone around,
And glory shone around.

"Fear not," said he,—for mighty dread
Had seized their troubled mind,
"Glad tidings of great joy I bring,
To you and all mankind,
To you and all mankind."

"To you in David's town this day,
Is born of David's line,
The Saviour, who is Christ, the Lord,
And this shall be the sign,
And this shall be the sign."

"The heav'nly babe you there shall find
To human view displayed,
All meanly wrapped in swathing bands,
And in a manger laid,
And in a manger laid."

Thus spake the seraph—and forthwith
Appeared a shining throng
Of angels, praising God, who thus
Addressed their joyful song,
Addressed their joyful song:—

"All glory be to God on high,

And to the earth be peace;
Good will henceforth, from heav'n to men,
Begin and never cease,
Begin and never cease."

The Prologue *appears before the curtains and speaks.*

Prologue.

There's scarlet holly on the streets, and silver mistletoe;
The surging, jeweled, ragged crowds forever come and go.
And here a silken woman laughs, and there a beggar asks—
And, oh, the faces, tense of lip, like mad and mocking masks.
Who thinks of Bethlehem today, and one lone winter night?
Who knows that in a manger-bed there breathed a Child of Light?

There's fragrant scent of evergreen upon the chilling air;
There's tinsel tawdriness revealed beneath the sunlight's glare;
There's Want and Plenty, Greed and Pride—a hundred thousand souls,
And, oh, the weary eyes of them, like dull and sullen coals.
Who knows the town of Bethlehem, once gleamed beneath the star,
Whose wondrous light the shepherds saw watching their flocks afar?

And yet above the city streets, above the noise and whir,
There seems to come a fragrant breath of frankincense and myrrh.
I saw a woman, bent and wan, and on her face a light
The look that Mary might have worn that other Christmas night.
And as the little children passed, and one lad turned and smiled,
I saw within his wistful eyes the spirit of the Child.
—*Caroline Reynolds.*

And there were in the same country shepherds abiding in the field, keeping watch over their flock by night. And, lo, the angel of the Lord came upon them, and the glory of the Lord shone round about them; and they were sore afraid.

And the angel said unto them, Fear not: for, behold, I bring you good tidings of great joy, which shall be to all people. For unto you is born this day in the city of David a Saviour, which is Christ the Lord.

And this shall be a sign unto you: Ye shall find the babe wrapped in swaddling clothes, lying in a manger.

And suddenly there was with the angel a multitude of the heavenly host praising God, and saying, Glory to God in the highest, and on earth peace, good will toward men.

And it came to pass, as the angels were gone away from them into heaven, the shepherds said one to another, Let us now go even unto Bethlehem, and see this thing which is come to pass, which the Lord hath made known to us.

And they came with haste, and found Mary and Joseph, and the babe lying in a manger. (*Exit* Prologue *at L.*)

(*Soft chimes are heard. The* Shepherds, *accompanied by the concealed choir, are heard singing:*)

LEAD, KINDLY LIGHT

Lead, kindly Light, amid th' encircling gloom,
Lead Thou me on!
The night is dark and I am far from home;
Lead Thou me on!
Keep Thou my feet, I do not ask to see
The distant scene; one step enough for me.

As the Shepherds *begin on the second stanza of the hymn, the curtains rise
disclosing the same scene as before.* Simeon, Timothy *and* Isaac *discovered
seated in a group at rear center, singing.* Thomas *stands by his father.*

So long Thy pow'r hath blest me, sure it still
Will lead me on
O'er moor and fen, o'er crag and torrent, till
The night is gone,
And with the morn those angel faces smile
Which I have loved long since, and lost a-while.

Simeon.
Methought I heard a whir of wings on high.

Timothy.
I see naught save the snow and starry sky.

Isaac.
We've come a long and mighty step today,
From o'er the frosty hills and far away.

Thomas (*pointing over the manger*).
Look, father, dost thou see that shining star
That seems to stand above the town so far?
'Tis like a wondrous blossom on a stem,
And see, it ever shines o'er Bethlehem!

Timothy.
A brighter star, I'm sure I never saw—
And perfect form, without a speck or flaw.

Simeon.
A stranger star! It never shone before,
It standeth still above that stable door.

Enter Anna *and* Ruth *from rear left.* Anna *carries a little lamb.*

Anna (*joining the group*).
Look ye, I've found a little lamb new-born.

Timothy.
Poor little beastie! Wrap him well and warm.

Simeon.
An ill night to be born in, frost and snow,
Naught but cold skies above, cold earth below.
I marvel any little creature should be born
On such a night.

Anna.
I found it all forlorn,
Crying beside its mother in the storm.

Simeon (*comes down a little to right front*).
Hark, I thought I heard a sound of mighty wings!
Listen! Is it the winter sky that sings?

Isaac (*with the group at rear center*).
Nay, gran'ther, I heard naught. You're old and gray
And weary with the miles you've walked today.

Simeon.
At noon I met a man who tarried in the shade,
He led a mule, and riding it a maid—
A maiden with a face I'll ne'er forget,
A wondrous face, I seem to see it yet
Lit with an inward shining, as if God
Had set a lighted lamp within her soul.
Many have passed all day, but none like these,
And no face have I ever seen like hers.

Timothy.
Belike the man and maid were strangers here,
And come to Bethlehem at the king's command.

Ruth (*comes down to* Simeon *and takes his hand*).
Methinks I met that very man and maid—
A maiden with such wondrous dove-like eyes,
I saw them near this place, all tired and worn,
Trudging about the town, seeking an inn.

Simeon.
And did they find one?

Ruth.
Nay, not so!
For every inn was crowded to its doors.
Hard by Deborah's inn there is a little barn,
All full of cattle, oxen, cooing doves—
I showed it to them, and they went therein.

Thomas (*standing at rear L. with* Anna).
Mother, that star! That wondrous, wondrous light,

(*Points up.*)

It turns the night to day, it shines so bright
I am afraid! It cannot be that any star,
Only a star, can give so great a light.
It frightens me.

Anna.
All things are strange tonight.
The very sheep are restless in their fold,
They watch the star and do not mind the cold.

Simeon (*puts hand to right ear, bends toward right and listens*).
Again I heard a singing in the sky!

Timothy.
You heard the tinkling bell of some stray sheep,
The night grows late, come let us all to sleep.

Simeon.
Yea, all ye lie down and take your rest,
I'll keep the watch alone, this night is blest.

(*The others recline at the rear.*)

Anna (*comes to* Simeon).
Here, take the little sheep and keep it warm.

(*Lies down.*)

Simeon.
Poor little new-born beast, I'll guard from harm.
Again I marvel that you should be born
On such a night, poor little lamb forlorn.

(Simeon *walks toward the manger with the sheep in his arms. The others sleep.*)

The Lord is my shepherd: I shall not want.

He maketh me to lie down in green pastures: he leadeth me beside the still waters.

He restoreth my soul: he leadeth me in the paths of righteousness for his name's sake.

Yea, though I walk through the valley of the shadow of death, I will fear no evil: for thou art with me; thy rod and thy staff they comfort me.

Thou preparest a table before me in the presence of mine enemies: thou anointest my head with oil; my cup runneth over.

Surely goodness and mercy shall follow me all the days of my life: and I will dwell in the house of the Lord for ever.

(*Soft Music.*)

Hark! There's music in the wind! And that strange light
There in the east, it brightens all the night!
I seem to hear again the whir of wings,
Awake, awake! It is an angel sings!

(*He arouses the others. They listen wonderingly, standing or reclining.*)

Voice (*an unseen soprano chants softly*).

Glory to God in the highest!
Fear not!
For behold I bring you glad tidings
Of great joy.
For unto you is born this day
In the city of David, a Saviour
Which is Christ, the Lord.
And this shall be the sign unto you:

Ye shall find the heavenly Babe
Wrapped in swaddling clothes,
Lying in a manger.
Glory to God in the highest,
And on earth peace,
Good will toward men!

Timothy.
'Twas a fine voice, even as ever I heard.

Anna.
The hills, as with lightning, shone at his word.

Simeon.
He spoke of a Babe here in Bethlehem.
That betokens yon star!
Full glad would I be,
Might I kneel on my knee,
Some word to say to that Child.

Timothy.
See! In the east there breaks the day.

Anna.
Let us tarry no longer; away, then, away!

(Anna *goes out at rear, behind the stable, with* Timothy, Ruth *and* Thomas.)

Isaac.
Come, gran'ther, let us go and see this thing!

Simeon.
But first get gifts to take the new-born King!
Glory to God in the highest,

And on earth peace,
Good will toward men.

(They follow the others out at rear.)

The curtains fall.

Scene III: *Hymn by the congregation:*

HARK! THE HERALD ANGELS SING.

Hark! The herald angels sing,
"Glory to the new-born King!
Peace on earth, and mercy mild,
God and sinners reconciled."
Joyful, all ye nations, rise,
Join the triumph of the skies;
With th' angelic host proclaim,
"Christ is born in Bethlehem."

Christ, by highest Heaven adored;
Christ, the everlasting Lord;
Late in time behold Him come,
Offspring of the favored one.
Veiled in flesh, the Godhead see;
Hail th' incarnate Deity:
Pleased, as man with men to dwell,
Jesus, our Immanuel.

Hail! The Heav'n-born Prince of Peace!
Hail! The Son of Righteousness!
Light and life to all He brings,
Risen with healing in His wings.
Mild He lays His glory by,
Born that man no more may die:
Born to raise the sons of earth,
Born to give them second birth.

Enter Prologue *before the closed curtains.*

Prologue.

Now when Jesus was born in Bethlehem of Judea in the days of Herod the king, behold, there came wise men from the east to Jerusalem, saying, Where is he that is born King of the Jews? For we have seen his star in the east, and are come to worship him.

When Herod the king had heard these things, he was troubled, and all Jerusalem with him. And when he had gathered all the chief priests and scribes of the people together, he demanded of them where Christ should be born.

And they said unto him, In Bethlehem of Judea: for thus it is written by the prophet, And thou Bethlehem, in the land of Juda, art not the least among the princes of Juda: for out of thee shall come a Governor, that shall rule my people Israel.

Then Herod, when he had privily called the wise men, inquired of them diligently what time the star appeared.

And he sent them to Bethlehem, and said, Go and search diligently for the young child; and when ye have found him, bring me word again, that I may come and worship him also.

When they had heard the king, they departed; and, lo, the star, which they saw in the east, went before them, till it came and stood over where the young child was.

When they saw the star, they rejoiced with exceeding great joy.

And when they were come into the house, they saw the young child with Mary his mother, and fell down, and worshipped him: and when they had opened their treasures, they presented unto him gifts; gold, and frankincense, and myrrh.

The White Christmas.

As the three wise men rode on that first Christmas night to find the manger-cradled Babe of Bethlehem, they bore gifts on their saddle-bows. Gifts of gold, frankincense and myrrh. And so the spirit of Christmas giving crept into the world's heart. We bring our gifts to the children. Rich children, poor children! The children of the high and the children of the humble! Poor little sick children—and the ragged children of the slums of our cities. Let us remember them all.

So go ye, all of ye, into the highways and byways, and seek out the poor and the distressed, the humble and the afflicted, seek out the ragged children and the outcasts and the aged ones, and in the name of Him who was born on Christmas day, carry some sunshine into their hearts! Give unto the poor and the afflicted, and your hearts shall glow with that inward peace that passeth all understanding.

Then—and then only—will you be able to sing with all the company of Heaven, Glory to God in the highest, peace on earth, good will toward men! And this will be your pure white Christmas. (*Exit* Prologue *at L.*)

Soft chimes are heard. The curtains are drawn, disclosing the same scene as before. Deborah *sits before her inn, deep in thought.*

Deborah (*reading a scroll*).

This is the ancient prophecy. Therefore the Lord himself shall give you a sign; behold, a virgin shall conceive, and bear a son, and shall call his name Immanuel.

Butter and honey shall he eat, that he may know to refuse the evil and choose the good.

For before the child shall know to refuse the evil, and choose the good, the land that thou abhorrest shall be forsaken of both her kings.

Enter Gaspar *from behind the inn. He comes down center.*

Gaspar.
I pray thee, tell me, Lady Bethlehemite,
If any wonders you have seen this night?

Deborah (*rises*).
I've seen a wondrous silver shaft of light
Come from a star, and blinded is my sight.

Gaspar.
Tell me, for thou art native of this place,
What dost thou know about the King of Grace—
King of the Jews?

Deborah.
Aye, in Jerusalem
He dwells, and not in Bethlehem.
He sits upon his mighty judgment throne,
Cruel and stern, his heart a living stone.

Gaspar.
I mean a new-born King, of love and peace;
His is the star—His reign shall never cease.

Deborah.
All things tonight seem passing strange to me,
I have just read an ancient prophecy
That this, our Bethlehem, King David's town,
Shall be the birthplace, e'er of great renown,
Of one called Councillor of King David's line
Whose coming is foretold in words divine.
And now you come with words of mystery!

(*Muses.*)

Why should thy questions, which are dark to me,
Cause me to think of Him?

Gaspar.

The star! The star!
No more it moves about the heavens afar,
It standeth still. O, hostess, kneel and pray,
For Jesus Christ, the Lord, is born today!

(*Hurries out right.*)

Deborah.
His words are fraught with mystery; I'll within
And seek protection in my humble inn.

(*Exits right front.*)

After a short pause, Melchoir, Gaspar *and* Baltasar *enter from rear right.*

Melchoir.

Three kings came riding from far away,
Melchoir, Gaspar and Baltasar;
Three wise men out of the east were they,
And they traveled by night and they slept by day,
For their guide was a beautiful, wonderful star.

Baltasar.

The star was so beautiful, large and clear,
That all other stars of the sky
Became a white mist in the atmosphere;
And by this they knew that the coming was near
Of the Prince foretold in prophecy.

Gaspar.

Of the child that is born, O Baltasar,
I begged a woman to tell us the news;
I said in the east we had seen His star,

And had ridden fast and had ridden far
To find and worship the King of the Jews.
—*Adapted from Longfellow.*

Melchoir.
Brothers, our quest is ended; see the star
Is standing still over this lowly hut.

Baltasar.
Methinks it is a stable. Knock and see!

Gaspar (*knocks on the door of the manger*).
What ho, within!

Joseph *enters from the L. rear.*

Joseph.
[Pg 36]Sirs, whom seek ye?

Melchoir.
We have journeyed from afar
Led by the shining of yon splendid star.
We are Gaspar, Melchoir and Baltasar.

Baltasar.
We seek a new-born King,
Gold, frankincense to him we bring.
And many a kingly offering.

Joseph *draws back the curtain and reveals the interior of the manger.* Mary *is seen bending over the crib. The* Shepherds *are kneeling in the background. Very soft music heard in the distance, with faintly chiming bells at intervals.*

Gaspar.
Behold, the child is clothed in light!

Melchoir.
Our journey ends, passed is the night.

Baltasar.
Now let us make no more delay,
But worship Him right worthily.

(*They enter the manger and kneel.*)

Simeon.
Hail, hail, dear child
Of a maiden meek and mild.
See, he merries!
See, he smiles, my sweeting,
I give thee greeting!
Have a bob of cherries.

(*Places a spray of cherries on the crib.*)

Timothy.
Hail, little One we've sought,
See, a bird I've brought,
See its feathers gay.
Hail, little One adored,
Hail, blessed King and Lord,
Star of the day!

(*Places a bird on the crib.*)

Isaac.
Hail, little One, so dear,
My heart is full of cheer,
A little ball I bring,

Reach forth thy fingers gay,
And take the ball and play,
My blessed King.

(Places a ball on the crib.)

Enter all others from the Inn. They kneel outside the manger.

All (*sing, with concealed choir*).

CHRISTMAS CAROL

Christ was born on Christmas day,
Wreathe the holly, twine the bay,
Light and life and joy is He—
The Babe, the Son,
The Holy One
Of Mary.

He is born to set us free;
He is born our Lord to be;
Carol, Christians, joyfully;
The God, the Lord,
By all adored
Forever.

Let the bright red berries glow,
Everywhere in goodly show,
Life and light and joy is He,
The Babe, the Son,
The Holy One
Of Mary.

Christian men, rejoice and sing;
'Tis the birthday of our King,
Carol, Christians, joyfully;
The God, the Lord,
By all adored
Forever.

The Three Kings.
Hail, King of Kings!

Gaspar.
I bring Thee a crown, O King of Kings,
And here a scepter full of gems,
For Thou shalt rule the hearts of men.

(*Places crown and scepter on crib.*)

Melchoir.
For Thee I bring sweet frankincense!

(*He swings a smoking censor.*)

Baltasar.
And I bring myrrh to offer Thee!

(*Places casket on the crib.*)

Gaspar.
The greatest gift is yet ungiven,
The gift that cometh straight from Heaven.
O, Heavenly King,
Heart's love we bring.

Melchoir.
Not gold nor gems from land or sea
Is worth the love we offer Thee.

Baltasar.
And lowly folk who have no gold,
Nor gift to offer that is meet,
May bring the dearest thing of all—
A loving heart and service sweet.

(All join in singing "Joy to the World.")

Curtain falls.

THE WHITE CHRISTMAS.

WHAT IT MEANS.

How to make a pleasant, *helpful* Christmas for the Sunday School is an annual problem. A tree with gifts, Santa Claus coming down the chimney, a treat of candy and nuts—these and many other schemes have been tried with a greater or less degree of success. But the criticism is often made that the true significance of the celebration of the birth of Christ is lost in the mere idea of bartering Christmas presents. "She didn't give me anything last year, so I'm not going to give her anything this year."

One wise superintendent determined to teach his Sunday School pupils the precious lesson of the beauty of giving. He called his teachers together a few weeks before Christmas and proposed to eliminate entirely the idea of "getting something," and in its stead to try to teach something of the true spirit of Christmas, the blessedness of giving.

The children were told that while at home they would receive all the usual presents, of course they would not get anything whatever from the Sunday School. The story of Jesus and how He gave His life, and how He liked best the gifts that cost us something, love, thought, foresight, charity, money— was told to the children and they were asked to save their pennies, instead of spending them for candy and nuts, to brighten the Christmas Day for God's poor and unfortunate.

It was put to a vote and every little hand was raised, although it may be confessed that a few went up a little reluctantly.

Teachers and young ladies met a few evenings later and made little stockings out of cheap cambric, with a cord put into the top of each in such a manner that it could be drawn together so the pennies would not be lost out. The stockings were about five inches long, and of various bright colors, and there were enough for every child. These were given out two weeks before Christmas.

On Christmas Eve, near the close of the regular program, a large tree was disclosed, but without a single present on it. The Minister made a short talk on the joys of giving to the poor and the children marched up, singing a Christmas carol, and attached their little stocking-bags to the tree.

Six little boys and girls passed among the congregation with larger stockings, collecting donations for the tree. These stockings had their tops neatly sewed around little circles of wire to keep them open.

The program consisted of Christmas hymns and carols, interspersed with recitations—all breathing the spirit of the White Christmas.

REMARKS ON THE PRODUCTION.

SCENERY.

Hang the rear and the sides of the stage with dark blue curtains, spangled
with small silver bits of tinfoil, to represent very tiny stars. If the blue
curtains are not available, use white sheets.

Cover the floor with white sheets. Have two or three small evergreen trees
at rear, covered with white calcimine and diamond powder. Soak long rags,
shaped like icicles, in a strong solution of alum, and then let them
crystallize, then attach them to the trees.

Down right, near the audience, is a doorway, supposed to be the entrance to
the inn. This may be simply an opening between two wooden columns, with

a step or two leading in. A lantern hangs over the door. A small bench stands by the inn.

Down left, near the audience, is the manger, a building extending out from left about seven feet. It has a back and one side of scenery or dark draperies and a thatched roof, covered with twigs or evergreen branches. There may be a door leading into the manger from the stage, but this is not necessary, as the characters can go out behind the manger. A front curtain, of dark goods, conceals the interior of the manger from the audience until it is withdrawn by Joseph.

The interior of the manger is covered with hay. Rude boxes and farm implements all around. A large upturned chair with wooden legs may simulate the crib, if it is concealed by enough straw. An electric light bulb is concealed in this straw and shines on the face of Mary, bending over the crib.

If desired, the manger scene may be presented in the choir loft, the manger hidden by curtains until revealed by Joseph. In this case have the evergreen trees at the left of the stage and arrange the manger scene at the rear and elevated above the other scene. This will prove most feasible in churches where the choir loft is immediately behind and above the platform.

LIGHTS.

Dim all the lights in the audience. Have a powerful searchlight, engine headlight or two powerful auto lights shining on the stage from a concealed elevation at the left. Shade these lights with a blue isinglass shield, thus casting a blue light over the entire stage. Use a strong yellow light on the manger scene, the rest of the stage being in darkness.

PROPERTIES.

If it is possible have bits of white confetti or finely cut paper fall from above during the shepherds' scene in Act II.

The bases of the trees should be covered with cotton.

Three rough crooks for the shepherds.

Chimes to ring off the stage. A dinner gong or set of chimes will answer.

For the lamb use a white muff, being careful to shield it from the direct gaze of the audience.

A spray of cherries.

A small bird of blue feathers.

A ball.

A crown and scepter made of gilded wood.

A censor made of metallic butter dish suspended by chains.

A fancy jewel case, supposed to contain myrrh.

Bench in front of inn.

Rude box in front of manger.

COSTUMES.

Mary—A sweet-faced blonde. Long tunic of light blue, falling straight from neck to the ankles. White stockings. Sandals. Hair in two long braids either side of face. White veil draped around head and shoulders, bound about the brow with circlet. Dark red mantle, fastened to left shoulder and draped around body. This mantle may trail on the ground. The tunic may be made of cotton crepon, the mantle of dyed muslin.

Joseph—A virile, bearded man of about fifty. Sandals. Long black cassock, easily obtained from an Episcopal choir. Striped couch cover may serve as mantle. This should be draped about head and body. Long staff.

Simeon—An old man with white hair and beard. Tunic of potato sacking falling in straight folds from neck to ankles. Large gray shawl serves as mantle, draped on head and body. Long crook. Sandals.

Timothy—Man of forty. Costume similar to Isaac's. Striped mantle.

Isaac—Man of twenty. Shorter tunic similar to Simeon's. Fur rug draped over left shoulder. Dark red drapery on head. Sandals. Brown stripes criss-crossed on legs. Crook.

Anna—Long tunic of brown. Take a square white sheet and stripe it with bands of dark blue. This serves as a mantle, draped over head and body. Hair hanging. A woman of thirty-five. Sandals. If desired, a blue veil may be draped around the head and neck and the mantle draped over the body.

Thomas—A boy of seven. Sandals. Brown strips criss-crossed on legs from sandals to hips. Short white tunic cut like a boy's nightgown, but coming only to knees. Dark blue mantle. Small crook.

Ruth—A girl of eleven. Blue tunic hanging in straight folds from neck to three or four inches above ankles. Border of figured goods, to simulate oriental embroidery, around bottom of robe and down the front. This should be about two inches wide. Sandals. White stockings. Hair hanging. White veil draped around head and shoulders. Later she enters with striped mantle.

Deborah—A dignified matron of about forty-five. Sandals. Long kimono of solid color. Sash of yellow. Hair in two long braids on either side of face. Yellow drapery over head and shoulders. Rich striped mantle draped over the costume.

Rachel—Sandals. White tunic trimmed with red figured cloth to simulate oriental embroidery. Red sash. Wreath of red roses on head. Mantle made of a square white sheet with stripes of red sewed on it. Bracelets, armlets and anklets of silver paper.

Priscilla—Sandals. Light green tunic. Dark green mantle. Gold paper armlets, etc.

Melchoir—Tall, dark man with dark mustache. Long black cassock may be borrowed from an Episcopal Church. Over this is a red or yellow kimono. Sandals. Turban on head. This turban may be made from a calico covered crown of an old derby, with red and white striped rim. He wears many rich ornaments. Curtain chains around neck and on arms. This costume may sometimes be borrowed from a lodge of Shriners, Knights Templar, Royal Arch Masons or Odd Fellows.

Gaspar—Similar to Melchoir. He is a young king aged about twenty-two. Wear white drapery on head and over it a golden (paper) crown. May wear sword. Sandals.

Baltasar—Old king with white hair. Long rich robe or kimono over a cassock. Red sash. Red head drapery. Golden crown. Sandals.

Angels—Invisible to the audience.

Prologue—Stately lady in trailing Grecian robe of white. Hair powdered. This character should be played by a lady with distinct dramatic ability.

Note.—If it is desired to simplify these costumes, kimonos, cassocks and cottas from Episcopal choirs, draperies of sheets and couch covers, and sandals made of a sole bound to foot with brown cloth cords, will answer admirably in the dim blue light.

Nightgowns, dressing gowns, fur rugs, fur muffs opened, fur stoles, opera capes, spangled tunics, window cords and chains, etc., will make valuable substitutes for the oriental garments.

ANITA'S SECRET OR CHRISTMAS IN THE STEERAGE

SANTA CLAUS · JACK FROST · ANITA · HULDA
SERGIUS · MEENY · BIDDY MARY · PADDY MIKE
TOMASSO · DUTCH TWINS · NEELDA · AH GOO
YAKOB · HANS · MIEZE · SANO SAN

ANITA'S SECRET OR CHRISTMAS IN THE STEERAGE

A CHRISTMAS PLAY IN ONE ACT FOR SANTA CLAUS AND SIXTEEN CHILDREN.

CHARACTERS.

Santa Claus	*Adult*
Jolly Jack Frost	*Little Boy*
Anita, *a Little Italian Immigrant*	*Aged Eight or Nine*
Hulda, *from Holland*	*Aged Ten*
Sergius, *from Russia*	*Aged Nine*
Meeny, *from Germany*	*Aged Seven*
Biddy Mary, *from Ireland*	*Aged about Eight*
Paddy Mike, *from Ireland*	*Aged about Seven*
Klinker	} *Little Dutch Twins*
Schwillie Willie Winkum	} *Aged Four or Five*
Neelda, *from Spain*	*Aged Five*
Ah Goo, *from China*	*Little Boy*
Yakob, *from Denmark*	*Aged Six*

Hans, *from Norway*   *Aged Four*

Mieze, *from Germany*   *Aged Six*

Sano San, *from Japan*   *Little Girl*

Time of Playing—*About One Hour and Fifteen Minutes.*

COSTUMES, ETC.

For notes on costuming, scenery and properties, see "Remarks on the Production of the Play" at the end of the play.

ARGUMENT.

It is the night before Christmas and the scene is on a big ocean-going vessel many miles out at sea. Down in the lower part of the ship, in the steerage, is a group of poor little immigrant children who are leaving the trials and troubles of the old world behind them and are looking forward to the golden promises held out by our own "land of the free and the home of the brave." But the hearts of the little immigrants are sad. It is the night before Christmas, and how could Santa Claus ever hope to reach them away out in the middle of the ocean? Even the sleigh and the magical reindeers could never be expected to make such a trip.

Anita, a little Italian girl, alone has faith in the coming of the good Saint. She is wandering around the ship when all of a sudden, much to her surprise, she hears a mysterious noise in a great big barrel, and who should jump out but little Jack Frost himself. Jack assures her that Santa Claus really is coming to visit the ship, and more than that, he is going to make an especial trip in an air ship! And this is little Anita's secret. The children all fall asleep, but Anita keeps watch for the mysterious aeroplane that will bring joy to every little heart in the steerage, and, sure enough, just a little before midnight Anita and Jack Frost look through a telescope and see the lights of the approaching air ship.

Soon Santa Claus himself is on board, and such a time as he and Anita and jolly Jack Frost have in arranging a wonderful Christmas surprise for the children. As an especial favor the good Saint decides to awaken the children himself very early on Christmas morning. The clock strikes twelve and it is Christmas Day. The bells of merry Christmas are heard chiming in the distance, and Santa Claus and jolly Jack Frost hold a Christmas morning revel with the little immigrant children away down in the steerage of the big vessel.

Scene: *The steerage of a large ocean-going vessel. Entrances R. and L. Boxes and barrels down L. Box down R. Large barrel up L.C., with* Jolly Jack Frost *concealed therein.* Hulda *is seated on a small stool down R., taking care of* Klinker *and* Schwillie Willie Winkum, *who are standing near her.* Meeny *is seated down L. on a box; she is knitting a woolen stocking.* Sergius, Paddy Mike, Tomasso, Yakob *and* Ah Goo *are playing leapfrog at C. of stage.* Hans, Mieze, Neelda *and* Sano San *stand at rear.* Biddy Mary *is seated near* Hulda; *she is peeling potatoes. All sing.*

OPENING SONG.

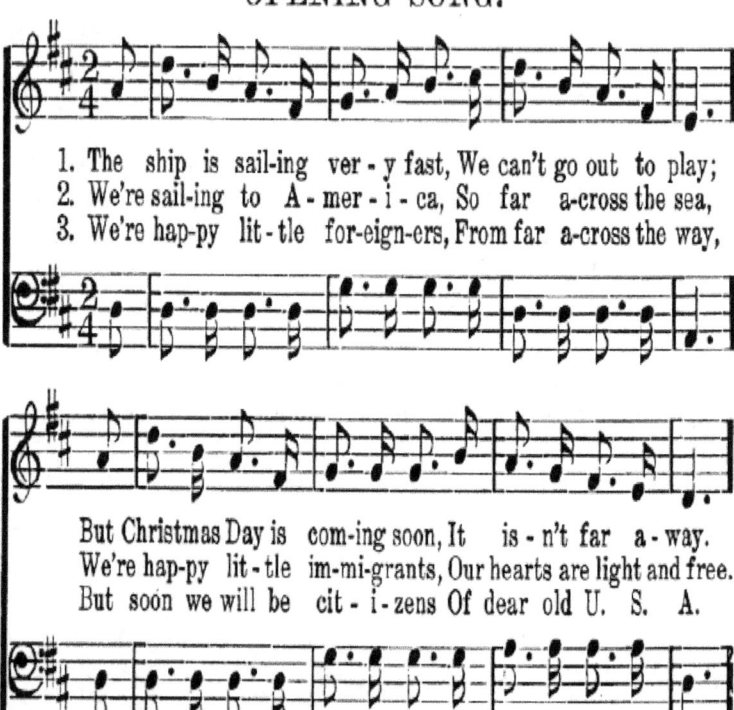

1. The ship is sail-ing ver-y fast, We can't go out to play;
2. We're sail-ing to A-mer-i-ca, So far a-cross the sea,
3. We're hap-py lit-tle for-eign-ers, From far a-cross the way,

But Christmas Day is com-ing soon, It is-n't far a-way.
We're hap-py lit-tle im-mi-grants, Our hearts are light and free.
But soon we will be cit-i-zens Of dear old U. S. A.

Then clap, clap, clap to-geth-er, Clap, clap, a - way;

The steer-age is a hap-py place—Tomorrow's Christmas Day.

(On the words "clap, clap, clap together," the children hold left hand horizontally in front of their chests, palm upward, raising the right hand and bringing it down on the left with a sharp clap.

Sing the first verse seated around stage. On the first four lines of the second verse nod heads and smile at audience. On the line "We're happy little immigrants," each one points to chest, nods head and smiles broadly.

For the third verse all rise and stand in couples in small groups all around stage. On the first two lines of the third verse each one faces his partner slightly, nods at him and shakes index finger of right hand at partner. On "dear, old U.S.A." all make a deep bow to audience. After third verse is completed, all form a circle and skip around in time to the music, repeating the third verse. On "clap, clap, clap together," they stand still and clap hands as before. When the song is ended all resume former positions, as at the rise of the curtain, but the boys do not play leapfrog.)

Tomasso (*seated on floor at C.*). Tomorrow comes the great, grand festival of Christmas, is it not, Paddy Mike?

Paddy Mike (*seated near him, nods his head*). Sure and it is. This is the holy Christmas Eve.

Meeny (*seated down L., knitting stocking*). The night of the day behind Christmas is always Christmas Eve, ain't it? (*Nods head.*) Sure it is.

Schwillie. Und tomorrow we gets lots of Christmas presents always, me und Klinker; don't we, Klinker?

Klinker. Sure we do. Leedle horses and pictures und candy und other things also; don't we, Schwillie Willie Winkum?

Hulda. That was when we were at home in Holland. It's different, maybe, out here in this great big boat. Ven we get by the city of New York next week then maybe we'll get some presents already.

Klinker. But good Saint Nicholas always comes the night before Christmas; don't he, Schwillie Willie Winkum?

Schwillie. Sure. Won't he come tonight, Hulda?

Hulda. How could he get way out here on the ocean already? Do you think he is a fish? We ain't living at home in Holland no more. We're way out on the Atlantic Ocean in a great big ship.

Meeny. Ja, und I wish I was back at home already. So much have I been seasick, mit der ship going oop und down, oop und down! Ach, it's awful. (Sergius, Tomasso, Yakob, Paddy Mike *and* Ah Goo *play jack-stones.*)

Klinker. But Saint Nicholas ought to come tonight, Hulda. I been a awfully good boy, isn't I, Schwillie Willie Winkum?

Schwillie. Sure you is. Und I've been a awfully good boy, too. Isn't I, Klinker?

Klinker. Sure. We've been awfully good boys.

Hulda. Maybe even if Saint Nicholas don't come tonight, you can see the great, big whale tomorrow. If he's a good whale he'll surely let the leedle Dutch twins see him on Christmas Day.

Meeny. Oh, I vant to see der whale. I've looked und I've looked und I've looked, but I ain't even so much as seen his leedle tail yet already. Und it makes me seasick to look so much, too.

Biddy Mary. Are ye sure it was a whale ye saw that day, Sergius boy?

Sergius. Of course I'm sure. It was awful big. The biggest fish I ever saw. Even in Russia we do not have such big fish as whales. Paddy Mike saw it, too.

Paddy Mike. Sure and I did. And me two eyes nearly fell out of me head with lookin' at it, it was that wonderful. He shot a big stream of water right up out of his head, he did, and then he dived down in the ocean again, and we didn't see him any more at all, at all. (Mieze *and* Sano San *turn backs to audience and look over the railing into the water.*)

Hulda (*to the twins*). There! Now if you get to see the great big whale, that's almost as good as having old Saint Nicholas come, ain't it?

Schwillie. Whales can't bring you no Christmas presents, can they, Klinker?

Klinker. Und whales you can see any time. I'd rather have Saint Nicholas, wouldn't I, Schwillie Willie Winkum?

Sergius. Who is this Saint Nicholas they are looking for, Hulda?

Hulda (*astonished*). Why, don't you know who he is yet? He's the best old man that ever was. Und he comes the night before Christmas und visits all the little children in Holland.

Meeny (*proudly*). Und in Germany, too. (Sergius *goes to* Hulda.)

Klinker. Und if they're good they get candy und oranges und toys und things, don't they, Schwillie Willie Winkum?

Schwillie. Und if they're bad, they get a good big birch stick. But I ain't been bad. I've been awfully good, isn't I, Klinker?

Klinker. Sure. Und me also.

Hulda (*to* Sergius). On Christmas Eve in Holland all the children march around the streets, following one who carries a big silver star. And the people who meet us give us money and gifts to help the poor. Oh, Christmas time is just grand in Holland!

Klinker. Und we set out our leedle wooden shoes und old Saint Nicholas fills 'em with candy.

Schwillie. Und we put a leedle bit of hay in our shoes for his good old horsie, Sleipner. Dot makes him happy.

Meeny. In Germany we call him Santa Claus, und he comes riding in a sleigh drawn through the sky mit reindeers. Und we have Christmas trees all lighted mit candles und things, und full of toys und paper stars und angels und apples. But Santa Claus could never get out here in der middle of der ocean. If he did maybe he'd get seasick already, und all der reindeers would get drownded in der water.

Sergius (*standing R.C.*). In Russia there is an old woman named Babouska who visits all the children on the night before Christmas. She carries a big basket full of good things.

Tomasso (*seated on floor at C.*). In sunny Italy the children all go to midnight church on Christmas Eve, and when we make ourselves awake on Christmas morning, our shoes are all full of candy and chestnuts and figs and oranges. But of course on a big ship like-a this we'll not get-a nothing at all.

Klinker (*crying*). But I want some presents already.

Schwillie (*crying*). Und me also. I want some presents, too.

Klinker. Und Saint Nicholas can't come. Oh, oh! He can't get out on the big ocean.

Schwillie. Maybe he could float out on a piece of ice yet. Could he, Hulda?

Hulda. No. I don't think he's much of a floater.

Meeny. If he did it would make him awful seasick.

Klinker. I wish we was landed in New York yet, so I do.

Schwillie. Where is Anita? She'll know.

Hulda. Yes, Anita will know whether he is coming or not. She knows almost everything.

Paddy Mike (*standing at rear L.*). Here comes Anita now, and sure she's having a grand time, so she is.

All (*rising and going to rear, looking off L.*). Here she comes. Hurrah for Anita. (*Music: The same as for the Opening Song.*)

Tomasso (*calling*). Anita, Anita, come here quick. We want you.

Anita (*outside L.*). I'm coming. Wait a minute. I'm coming.

Music swells louder. Anita *dances in from L., all sing as she dances around, waving her tambourine.*

All (*singing to tune of the "Opening Song"*).

We're sailing to America,
Away across the sea,
We're happy little immigrants,
Our hearts are light and free.
Then clap, clap, clap together,

(*All skip around.*)
Clap, clap away;
The steerage is a happy place—
Tomorrow's Christmas Day.

Anita (*comes forward to C. surrounded by the others*). Oh, I've just had the grandest time. It was so superb, magnificent, sublime! (*Extends arms in ecstasy.*) I have-a been at the leetla window watching the great, grand, magnificent ocean. It was all so blue and so green and so purple—and the sinking sun is all shining on the great-a, beeg waves, like-a sparkling diamonds. (*Use elaborate gestures at all times.*) And me, the poor, leetla Italian girl, gets to see all this great-a, grand-a ocean. It is superb, magnificent, sublime! Ah, I am so happy, I could sing and dance and kees everybody on the great-a, grand-a earth!

Meeny (*at L.*). Vot makes you so happy, Anita? Maybe I'd be happy yet also, if I didn't get seasick once in a while.

Anita. What makes me so happy, Meeny? It's the sun and the waves, and the sunlight shining like diamonds on the great-a, grand-a ocean. Are you not also happy, Biddy Mary?

Biddy Mary (*standing by* Anita). I am not. Sure, I niver do be having time to be seeing diamonds on the great big waves. I have to be hard at work, so I do, peeling the praties for our Christmas breakfast.

Anita. I watched the great-a red sun as he began to sink, sink, sink way down in the ocean. And the beeg-a waves got more beeg and more beeg and on top of them I saw long white lace fringe. The green silk waves were all-a trimmed with white lace fringe. And sometimes I think I see the leetla mermaid fairies dancing in the foam. Leetla green and white mermaids with the long long-a hair.

Tomasso (*at R.*). You make-a me seek, Anita. There is-a no such things as fairies.

Anita. But I love to *think* there is. It is a great, grand-a pleasure just to think there is. Is it not, Meeny?

Meeny (*stolidly*). Oh, sure.

Anita. And that is why we should all be so verra, verra happy. We can think such-a lovely things. The poor leetla children at-a home, pouf! They cannot think such things, because they have never seen such a great, beeg-a ship, or such a great, beeg-a ocean—

Sergius. Or a whale.

Paddy Mike. Or a sailor man.

Hulda. Or a nice little steerage bed built just like a shelf in the wall.

Tomasso. Or the great beeg-a engine that makes the ship go.

Meeny. Or the tons and tons of coal vay down deep by the cellar.

Sergius (*mocking her*). Way down deep by the cellar! Whoever heard of a cellar on board of a ship? You mean—down in the hatch.

Meeny. Hatch? Vot is dot hatch? Dis ain't a chicken, it's a boat. (*All laugh.*)

Klinker (*takes* Schwillie *by the hand and goes to* Anita). Anita, we want to ask you a question.

Anita. Well, and what is the question of the leetla Dutch twins?

Schwillie. Tonight is the night before Christmas.

Klinker. Und we want to know if the good Saint Nicholas is coming tonight.

Anita. I don't know. You see it would be a great beeg-a, long-a trip way out here on the ocean.

Klinker (*half crying*). But I want him to come. I've been a awful good boy, isn't I, Schwillie Willie Winkum?

Schwillie. Sure, you is. Und me also, ain't I, Klinker?

Anita. If you have both been verra, verra good I think that maybe the good Saint will come. (*Looks around.*) Have you all been verra, verra good?

Others. Yes, all of us.

Hans. We're always very, very good at Christmas time.

Ah Goo. Me velly, *velly* good.

Anita (*points off R.*). See, way up there on the upper deck, are the rich, grand-a ladies and gentlemen coming out from the great, beeg-a dining-room. If you go and stand under the hole maybe they'll throw you some oranges or candy. They're awful nice peoples on the upper deck.

Meeny. Let's all go right away quick. Maybe we'll get some oranges und candy.

Klinker. Oh, how I do love oranges und candy, don't I, Schwillie Willie Winkum?

Schwillie. Sure, und me also, don't I, Klinker?

Sergius. Let us all go together. (*All come forward and sing to tune of the Opening Song.*)

We're happy little immigrants,
We'll sing our happy song,
Our hearts are light, our faces bright—
The good ship speeds along.
Then clap, clap, clap together,
Clap, clap away;
The steerage is a happy place—

Tomorrow's Christmas Day.

(All the children except Anita *go out at R., repeating the chorus of their song.)*

Anita. Surely the good-a Saint Nicholas will come tonight, because there are so many, many verra good children on board this-a ship. (*Counting on fingers.*) There's Hulda from Holland and her two leetla brothers, the Dutch twins, Klinker and Schwillie Willie Winkum. They must have a great-a beeg-a Christmas present. And there's Sergius from Russia, and Meeny and Paddy Mike and Biddy Mary, and Neelda from Spain, and Yakob and Hans and Ah Goo and Mieze and leetla Sano San from afar away Japan. They must all have the great-a, grand-a presents. Maybe I could write old Santa Claus a leetla letter and tell how good the poor children way down in the steerage have been. And there's my cousin Tomasso from Italy. Oh, Santa Claus must bring him a new violin. Then he can make-a the beautiful music on the golden streets of New York. If there is anybody at all in the whole beeg world who should have a nice-a, beeg-a Christmas, it is the verra poor leetla children whose mammas and papas haven't got very much money. But sometimes the good Santa Claus forgets all about the verra poor leetla children—and that's the mostest saddest thing of all, for they are the verra ones he should remember. When I get to be a great-a, beeg, grand-a, reech lady in the golden streets of New York, ah! then I will buy presents and presents and presents, and I will-a give them to all the verra poor leetla children in the world. I wonder why it is that the verra good Santa Claus sometimes forgets the poor leetla children on-a Christmas Day. He never forgets the reech leetla children, only those who are verra, verra poor. And that is a sad misfortune. If I had-a nice-a Christmas present, with many candies and figs and oranges, I could never rest until I had given something nice to all the poor leetla children in the city—for that is what makes the mostest happy Christmas of all.

Enter Sergius *from R. quietly. He comes down behind* Anita *and places his hands over her eyes.*

Sergius. Guess who it is.

Anita. Sergius!

Sergius (*disappointed*). Why, I thought that you would think it was a goblin.

Anita. Goblin? What is a goblin, Sergius?

Sergius. It's a little, wee bit of a man with a long beard. And they go around having a good time at night. They are always very active on the night before Christmas. (*Looks cautiously around.*) I shouldn't be at all surprised if we should see some tonight.

Anita (*frightened*). Oh, Sergius, will they harm us?

Sergius. Not very much. They just like to have a little fun, that's all. We have lots of them in Russia. And I believe there are some down here in the steerage.

Anita (*grasps his arm*). Oh, Sergius! Where are they?

Sergius. Well, last night I could not sleep, so I got up and came in here, and just as I was passing by that barrel (*points to barrel up L.C. where* Jack Frost *is concealed*), I thought I heard a noise. It was like some one rapping on the barrel. Like this. (*Raps on another barrel.*) I thought it was a goblin and I never stopped running until I was safe in my bunk with the bedclothes around my head.

Anita. Pooh! I'm not afraid. No leetla goblin man can make-a me afraid.

Sergius. They do wonderful things on Christmas Eve. But come; let us go to the bottom of the stairs. The ladies and gentlemen are looking down and Tomasso is playing his violin. Soon they will throw apples and oranges down to us, and perhaps money. Come and see.

Anita. No, I'd rather wait here.

Sergius (*crossing to door at R.*). All right, but don't let the goblin man catch you. (*Exits at R.*) Anita. The goblin man! Poof! There is no such thing as a goblin man. In-a Italy we do not have such goblin mans. He said he heard something rap, rap on the inside of the barrel. Poof! Sergius must have been having one beeg, grand-a dream. Never in all my life did I ever hear anything go rap, rap on the inside of a barrel. (*Stands close to* Jack Frost's *barrel.*) And if I did, I'd think it was a leetla, weeny-teeny mouse. But a leetla, weeny-teeny mouse never could go rap, rap on the inside of a barrel, try as hard as he could. It must have been a dream.

Jack Frost (*raps sharply on the inside of the barrel*).

Anita. Oh, what was that? I thought I heard something. (*Goes toward barrel cautiously.*) Maybe it is the leetla, teeny-weeny baby mouse. (Rises on tiptoes to peer into the barrel.) I'll just peek in and see. (*Just as she looks into the barrel,* Jack Frost *pops up his head almost in her very face.*)

Jack Frost. Hello!

Anita (*starting back, very much frightened*). Oh!

Jack Frost. Did you say oh, or hello?

Anita. I just said, oh.

Jack Frost. Well, then, hello. (*Climbs out of the barrel.*)

Anita. Hello.

Jack Frost (*goes to her*). You aren't frightened, are you?

Anita (*at R.*). Well, I'm a leetla frightened, but not verra much.

Jack Frost. Why? I won't hurt you.

Anita. You came up so sudden. I never expected[Pg 64] to find a boy in that barrel. And you are such a queer looking boy.

Jack Frost. Boy? I'm not a boy.

Anita. You're not? You look like a boy. You're not a girl, are you?

Jack Frost (*indignantly*). Well, I should say not! I'm just a kind of a sort of a kind of an idea, that's all. I'm your imagination.

Anita. I hope you're not a goblin.

Jack Frost. Oh, no. I'm not a goblin. They're old and have long beards. I'm not old at all. (*Twirls around on toes.*) See, I'm even younger than you are. (*Makes low bow.*) I'm a pixie.

Anita. And what is a pixie?

Jack Frost. I told you before, it's just your imagination.

Anita. You look like a boy. What is your name?

Jack Frost. My name is Claus.

Anita. Claus! Why, what a funny leetla name. I never heard a name like that in Italy. Claus what?

Jack Frost. Santa Claus. Haven't you ever heard of Santa Claus?

Anita. Oh, yes; many, many times. But you *can't* be Santa Claus.

Jack Frost (*indignantly*). I'd like to know why I can't! It's my name, isn't it?

Anita. But you are not the real, real truly Santa Claus. He is an old, old man. A leetla fat old man with white-a hair just like-a the snow, and a long, white-a beard.

Jack Frost. Ho, you must be thinking of my daddy.

Anita. Your daddy? Is Santa Claus your daddy?

Jack Frost. Sure, he is. I'm Jack Frost Santa Claus, Jr. Most folks call me Jolly Jack Frost. The little fat man with the white beard is my father.

Anita (*astonished*). Why, I didn't know Santa Claus had any leetla boys.

Jack Frost. Sure, he has. Who do you think takes care of the reindeer, and who waters the doll-tree and picks the dolls?

Anita. Picks the dolls? Do the dolls grow on trees?

Jack Frost. Yes, indeed, right next door to the taffy cottage, down Chocolate Lane. I take care of the marble bushes and the popgun trees. You just ought to see our wonderful gardens.

Anita. Oh, I'd love to see them.

Jack Frost. We've got a Teddy-bear garden, and a tool garden, and a furniture garden, and a game garden, and a candy garden, though most of the candy comes from mines.

Anita. The mines?

Jack Frost. Sure. We dig out just the kind we want. We have caramel mines, and vanilla mines and mines full of chocolate almonds, and rivers of fig paste and strawberry ice cream soda. They flow right through the picture-book garden.

Anita. Oh, it must be the most wonderful place in the whole world.

Jack Frost. And I help take care of it. I have fourteen little brothers, and we're all twins.

Anita. And have you a mother, too? Has Santa Claus a nice-a, fine-a wife?

Jack Frost (*laughs*). Of course he's got a wife. Haven't you ever heard of my mother. Her name is Mary.

Anita. Mary? Mary what?

Jack Frost. Why, Merry Mary Christmas, of course. I thought everyone knew that.

Anita. And does she go round the world with Santa Claus on the night before Christmas?

Jack Frost. Oh, no, she's too busy for that. She stays at home and takes care of the gardens.

Anita. But what are you doing here on the ship? I should think you'd be with your father.

Jack Frost. Ah, that is a secret. You mustn't tell anyone.

Anita. How can I tell anyone when I don't know myself.

Jack Frost. Well, maybe I'll tell you.

Anita. Oh, if you only would. I'd just love to have a great-a, beeg, grand-a secret.

Jack Frost. You can keep a secret, can't you?

Anita. Of course I can. Girls can always keep secrets.

Jack Frost. Some girls can't. But I believe you really can. Your name's Anita, isn't it?

Anita. Yes. But how did you know?

Jack Frost. Oh, we know everything. How old are you?

Anita. If you tell me how you knew my name, I'll tell you how old I am.

Jack Frost. Well, I just guessed it.

Anita. Then why don't you guess how old I am?

Jack Frost. Cute, ain't you?

Anita. Not so verra cute. I'm going on nine.

Jack Frost. Then you're old enough to keep the secret. Now, first you must promise you won't tell until tomorrow morning.

Anita. Cross my heart. (*She does so.*)

Jack Frost (*crosses to her*). Listen, then; here's the secret. (*He whispers in her ear.*)

Anita (*after a pause, while he is whispering*). He is? *He is?* Oh!!

Jack Frost (*nods his head wisely*). Yes, he is.

Anita. Honest?

Jack Frost. Honest injun!

Anita. With his pack and presents and a Christmas tree and everything?

Jack Frost (*nods head emphatically*). Yes, ma'am, every single thing.

Anita. Tonight?

Jack Frost. Just before the clock strikes twelve, when all the little children in the steerage are asleep.

Anita. But how will he get out here in the middle of the ocean?

Jack Frost. Fly.

Anita. Fly? But he hasn't any wings. (Jack *nods.*) He has? (Jack *nods.*) Really and truly wings?

Jack Frost (*nods*). Really and truly wings.

Anita. I never knew Santa Claus had wings before.

Jack Frost. He only bought them this year.

Anita. Bought them? (Jack *nods.*) Then they didn't grow on him?

Jack Frost (*laughs*). Of course not. He's coming in an air ship.

Anita. Why, I never knew Santa Claus had an air ship.

Jack Frost. He's got the very latest twentieth century model. He only uses the reindeer once in a while now. He can go much faster on an air ship. (*Sits down.*) Oh, I'm tired.

Anita. I didn't know pixies ever got tired.

Jack Frost. You ought to see the work I've done today.

Anita. Here on the boat?

Jack Frost. Yes, ma'am, right here on the boat.

Anita. Oh, show me.

Jack Frost. I will. But it's part of the secret. (*Goes to rear L.*) Come here and I'll show you what I've been doing.

Anita (*goes to him*). It isn't anything scary, is it?

Jack Frost. Of course not. (*Lets her peep through the curtain that conceals the Christmas tree from the audience.*) There; what do you think of that?

Anita. Oh, oh! oh!! It's too great and grand and wonderful for words. Oh, what a wonderful, wonderful secret! I'm so glad you've told me. It is so much nicer to know all about it beforehand. I wish I could tell Tomasso.

Jack Frost. Well, you can't. It's a secret and you mustn't tell anybody.

Anita. But are you really, truly sure he's coming?

Jack Frost. Of course he is. That is our secret.

Anita. Oh, it's the grandest secret I ever had in all-a my life. I will not tell a soul that he is-a coming. It will be a Christmas surprise, and when I get to the beeg city of New York in America, I'll always remember this great-a beeg, nice-a secret about old Santa Claus and his nice leetla boy, Jack Frost.

Jack Frost. What are you going to do when you get to America?

Anita. I am going to dance. My uncle, Pedro Spanilli, he haba de grind-organ. Until last-a month he had-a de nice-a monkey, named Mr. Jocko, but last-a month Mr. Jocko he die, and my uncle, Pedro Spanilli, he send for me to take-a his place.

Jack Frost. Take the monkey's place?

Anita. Yes, sir. I'm going to go round with my uncle and hold out my tambourine, so! (*Poses and holds out tambourine.*) And then I will-a collect the pennies, just like-a Mr. Jocko used to do.

Jack Frost (*mocking her*). I suppose you are going to wear a leetla red cap and jump up and down this way (*imitates a monkey*), and say, "Give-a de monk de cent!"

Anita (*laughing*). Oh, no. I'm going to sing the leetla song, and dance the leetla dance, so! (*Hums and dances, or a song may be introduced at this point by* Anita.) Then, when I'm finished, I go to the kind leetla boy, Jack Frost, and hold out my tambourine, so! (*Does so.*) And maybe he drops a nickel in my tambourine. Eh? Does he?

Jack Frost (*sighs, then drops a nickel in tambourine*). Yes, I guess he does. And you just wait till tomorrow morning, Anita, and I'll give you the finest Christmas present on the Atlantic Ocean.

Anita. And you must not forget the leetla Dutch twins, and my cousin Tomasso, and Hulda and Meeny and Sergius and Ah Goo and Sano San and Needla and Biddy Mary and Paddy Mike and all the rest.

Jack Frost. Whew! That's a big order. But we won't forget a single soul on Christmas Day. And now I've got to go and put the finishing touches on— you know what! (*Goes behind curtains that conceal the Christmas tree.*)

Anita (*looks around*). Why, he's gone.

Jack Frost (*sticking his head out of the curtains*). The sun has set, it's out of sight, so little Jack Frost will say good-night! (*Disappears back of curtains.*)

Anita. Good-night, Jolly Jack Frost, good-night. Oh, it's the most wonderful secret in all the world. And won't the leetla children be glad to know that old Santa Claus has not forgotten them. He said that Santa Claus was coming tonight in the air ship, and it's got to be true, it's just got to be true.

Enter Tomasso *from R., carrying violin.*

Tomasso. Anita, if you don't hurry you'll not get any supper at all. It's most eight o'clock.

Anita. Oh, I don't care for supper, Tomasso. I could-a not eat. I'm too much excited to eat.

Tomasso. What make-a you so excited, Anita?

Anita. Why, tonight—(pauses as she remembers her promise) Oh, that I cannot tell; it's a secret.

Tomasso. What is the secret?

Anita. If I told-a you, Tomasso, then it would no longer be a secret.

Tomasso. You should-a not have the secrets from me, Anita. I am your cousin, also—I am the head of the family.

Anita. But I made the promise not to tell.

Tomasso. Who you make-a the promise to?

Anita. I promised Jack—(*hesitates*) I mean, I make-a de promise to someone.

Tomasso. To Jack! Who is this-a Jack, Anita?

Anita. That is part of the secret. Listen, Tomasso, tomorrow morning you shall know everything. Early in the morning shall I tell-a you my secret. That will be my Christmas present to you.

Tomasso. All right. I'll wait. Oh, see, Anita, the moon is coming up. (*Points to L.*) Just like-a big, round-a silver ball.

Anita. Let us stay here and watch the moon, Tomasso.

Tomasso. You'd better go and get your supper. Those leetla Dutch twins are eating everything on the table. I think they'd eat the table itself if it was-a not nailed to the deck. Hurry, Anita!

Anita. I go. (*Crosses to door at R., then turns toward him*). It's a awful good-a secret, Tomasso. (*Laughs and runs out at R.*)

Tomasso (*looks off L.*). Ah, the great, grand-a lady moon. She looks at me, I look at her. Maybe she'll like a leetla serenade.

(*Simple violin solo by* Tomasso, *accompanied by hidden organ or piano. After he has been playing sometime, the other children come softly in from the R. and group around the stage. Note: If possible, get a boy for* Tomasso's *part who can play the violin; if not, introduce a song at this point. "Santa Lucia," found in most school collections, would prove effective either as a vocal solo or as a violin solo.*)

Biddy Mary. Sure, that's beautiful. It takes me back again to dear ould Ireland where the River Shannon flows.

Hulda. What do you do in Ireland the night before Christmas, Biddy Mary?

Meeny. Do you have a Christmas tree like we do in Germany?

Biddy Mary. We do not. We don't have any tree at all, at all.

Paddy Mike. And we don't get many presents. But it's a fine time we have for all that. Instead of getting presents, we have the fun of giving presents— and that's the finest thing in all the world, so it is, to make the other fellow happy. Sure, I just love to give presents.

Klinker. You can give me some if you want to.

Schwillie. Und me also some.

Biddy Mary. But where would we be getting presents out here in the middle of the ocean? In dear ould Ireland sure it's a fine time we're after having on Christmas Day.

Paddy Mike. It is that. With the fiddles playing and the dancers dancing and the fine suppers upon the table.

Sergius. In Russia we always set a table in front of the window and put a fine linen cloth on it. (*Produces white lace-edged cloth.*) Here is the cloth, but we have no window.

Hulda. Here, use this box as a table. (*Indicates a large box at rear C.*) Now, let us put the cloth on, so! (Hulda *and* Sergius *put cloth on the box.*)

Biddy Mary. The night before Christmas we always put a big candle, all gay with ribbons, in the window to welcome the Christ child.

Paddy Mike. Here is the candle. (*Places it on box at rear C.*) Now I'll light it. (*Lights candle.*)

Tomasso. We do that also in Italy. And we put a leetla picture of the Christ child on the table. (*Puts colored picture of Madonna and Child back of the candle.*)

Biddy Mary. On Christmas Day it's the fine old tales we're after hearing in Ireland, all about the wonderful star that shone so bright that it turned night into day, and led the Wise Men all the way to where a little Babe in the manger lay.

Paddy Mike. And all the angels sang above of peace on earth, good will and love.

Biddy Mary.

The shepherds wandering on the hill,
Beheld the star and followed till
They saw the Child and heard the song,
The angels sang the whole night long.

Sergius. May the spirit of Christmas enter every heart tonight, making all the world one big, happy family, no rich, no poor, no high, no low, all brothers and sisters, all children of the Lord on high!

Meeny. Maybe good old Santa Claus will come after all. Vell, if he does I want to be ready for him. (*Produces two very large red stockings, made for the occasion.*) Come, Yakob and Hans and Mieze, let us hang up our stockings here under the burning candle. (*They hang up the four pair of stockings.*)

Neelda (*places a wreath of holly on the table*). Christ was born on the Christmas Day, wreathe the holly, twine the bay! Light and Life and Joy is He, the Babe, the Son, the Holy One of Mary!

Tomasso. Meeny and Yakob and Hans and leetla Mieze have hung up their stockings for the good-a Saint Nicholas, but in Italy we set out our shoes, so! And we always get them full of presents. (*Places small pair of wooden shoes on table.*)

Meeny. I like stockings much better than shoes already, because the stockings can stretch yet, und if they stretch real, real wide out maybe we can get a baby piano or a automobile in our stockings. Jah, stockings is mooch better als shoes.

Hulda. Here is my beautiful star. (*Produces tinsel star.*) That will remind us of the Star of Bethlehem that led the three Wise Men across the hills and plains of Judea unto the little manger where, surrounded by cattle and oxen, amid the straw, the Lord of Heaven was born on Christmas Eve.

Schwillie. Und all the angels sang, "Peace on earth, good will to men," didn't they, Klinker?

Klinker. Und all the shepherds heard them, and they followed the star and came to the manger to see the little Baby.

Meeny. Let us all sit down here in front of the candle and the star, and see if old Santa Claus has forgotten us already. It's almost time for him to be coming. (*All sit down.*)

All (*sing*).

THE TIME IS NEAR.

1. The time is near, the time is near,
2. Be - fore the dawn, be - fore the dawn,

San - ta Claus will soon be here! All the world is
Saint Nick will have come and gone! Now with pa-tience

sweet-ly sleep-ing, An - gels now their watch are keep-ing,
we'll a - wait him, Hop - ing noth - ing may be - late him,

And   the moon shines clear,   And   the moon shines clear.
On   his jour - ney   long,   On   his jour - ney   long.

Hulda. Oh, I do hope Santa Claus will come and visit us tonight. But of course he cannot go every place. Some children have to be left out.

Klinker. Yes, that's so; but I hope it ain't us. Don't you, Schwillie Willie Winkum?

Schwillie. Sure, I do. I wish old Santa would hurry up and come, 'cause the old Sandman is here already. I'm getting awful sleepy.

Klinker. Me—I'm getting awful sleepy, too. (*Stretches and yawns.*)

Tomasso. I wonder what has become of Anita? She said she had a wonderful secret that was-a verra, verra grand.

Meeny. A secret, Tomasso? (*Goes to him.*)

Tomasso (*standing at C.*). Yes, a great, beeg, grand-a secret.

Biddy Mary (*goes to him and takes his L. arm*). Oh, what is it, Tomasso?

Meeny (*taking his R. arm*). Yes, Tomasso, tell us vot it is already.

Biddy Mary (*turning Tomasso around to face her*). Sure, if there's anything on earth I *do* love, it's a secret.

Hulda (*and the other girls, surrounding Tomasso*). Yes, Tomasso, tell us the secret; we'll never tell anyone.

Meeny (*pulling him around to face her*). Sure we won't. Nice Tomasso, tell us vot it is yet.

Tomasso (*hesitates*). Well, I——

Biddy Mary (*pulling him around to face her*). Now, you tell *me*, Tomasso. I never tell any secrets at all, at all.

Tomasso. Well, I——

Meeny (*pulls him around again*). If you're going to tell it, I want to hear every word. I never want to miss noddings no times.

Biddy Mary (*pulls him back*). Neither do I.

Hulda. Neither do I.

Meeny. Neither do any of us.

Klinker. I don't want to miss nothing neither.

Schwillie. No, und I don't neither.

All. Now, what is the secret, Tomasso?

Tomasso (*loudly*). It is not my secret. It is Anita's secret.

All. Well, what is Anita's secret.

Tomasso. She wouldn't tell me.

All (*turn away very much disappointed*). Oh!

Tomasso. She's promised to tell us all in the morning. She said that would be her Christmas present to us—to tell us the secret. (*All sit or recline around the stage. Lower the lights.*)

Sergius. It seems so strange to spend Christmas Eve away out here in the middle of the ocean.

Klinker (*almost asleep*). Wake me up, Hulda, just as soon as Santa Claus comes.

Biddy Mary (*at R.*). Sure I think the Sandman has been after spillin' sand in all of our eyes. I'm that sleepy I can't say a word at all, at all.

Sano San. They're putting out all the lights. Here, Sergius, hang my little lantern in front of the candle.

Ah Goo. Allee samee hang mine. (Sano San *and* Ah Goo *each give their lanterns to* Sergius, *who lights them and hangs them on the table. Note: Nails must be put in the table at R. and L. corners facing front for these lanterns.*)

Sergius. I'm going to stretch out here and take a little nap. (*Reclines on floor.*) Be sure and wake me up, Hulda, just as soon as you hear the bells on his reindeer.

Tomasso (*yawns*). I wonder what has become of Anita?

Hulda (*stretches*). I believe I'm getting sleepy, too.

Others. So are all of us.

Biddy Mary. We're all noddin', nid, nid noddin', sure I think it's time we were all of us fast asleep.

All (*sing sleepily*).[Pg 78]

"WE'RE ALL NODDIN'."

1. We are all nod - din', nid, nid nod - din', We are
2. We are all nod - din', nid, nid nod - din', We are

all nod - din', and drop - ping off to sleep.
all nod - din', and drop - ping off to sleep.

So see San - ta Claus we've all done our best,
It's aw - ful - ly late, we'll no lon - ger de - lay,

But we're aw - ful - ly sleep-y, so we'll take a rest.
But ride with the Sand-man, a - way and a - way.

Transcriber's Note: Two musical errors, both in the last bar, have been corrected in the MIDI file: the second G in the treble staff should be natural; and the second B in the bass staff should be a C. In the lyrics, the word "So" in bar 6 should probably be "To."

(All *are sound asleep. Stage is dark.*)

Klinker (*talking in his sleep*). Noddin', nid, nid noddin'.

Schwillie (talking in his sleep). Dropping off to sleep, ain't we, Klinker?

Soft, mysterious music. Anita *dances in from R. She dances around the stage, keeping time to the music and bending over the little sleepers.*

Anita. Asleep! Every last one of them is verra sound asleep. Meeny and Biddy Mary, and Sergius and Tomasso and the leetla Dutch twins and all! (*Goes to curtain at rear.*) Jack Frost! Jolly Jack Frost! Come-a quick, come-a quick! They're all asleep.

Jack Frost (*sticks his head out of the curtains*). Hello, what is it?

Anita. It is Anita. The leetla children are all here and sound asleep.

Jack Frost (*coming down to her*). And so was I. They sang a song about noddin', nid, nid noddin', and I just went to sleep myself. I dreamed I was hunting a polar bear way up by the North Pole. (*Yawns.*) I'm still awfully sleepy.

Anita. I didn't know that you ever went to sleep.

Jack Frost. You bet I do. That's the one thing I've got against my daddy's Christmas trip every year. It wakes us all up right in the middle of the night.

Anita. The middle of the night? What *do* you mean?

Jack Frost. Middle of the north pole night. If it wasn't for Christmas we could go to bed about half past October and sleep until a quarter of May, but ma thinks we ought to help pa and then wait up until he comes home. My, I'm sleepy! Aren't you?

Anita. Oh, no, no! I'm verra too much excited to sleep. It's all about my secret. Are you really sure he is coming?

Jack Frost. Of course he is, and it's almost time he was here now. It's nearly Christmas Day. Look way up there in the sky. You don't see anything that looks like an air ship, do you?

Anita (*looking up and off at R.*). No, I cannot see a single thing.

Jack Frost (*sees table at rear*). Oh, look here! The children have lighted a candle for him. That's just fine. It always pleases him. And see; here's a picture and a wreath of holly and the star of Bethlehem. And stockings and shoes all in a row.

Anita (*looking up and off R.*). I can't see a thing.

Jack Frost. Here's a telescope. Look through that. (*Takes home-made telescope from his barrel.*) Now do you see anything?

Anita. Oh, no; now I cannot even see the stars or the moon.

Jack Frost. Of course you can't. You are looking through the wrong end. Turn it around.

Anita (*looks up and off R. through telescope*). Oh, now I can see the stars. And, oh, look! I see a leetla, teeny-weeny thing way, way off—far up in the sky. Look, Jack Frost, is that the air ship?

(*Fast music, played softly.*)

Jack Frost (*looks through the telescope*). Yes, I believe it is.

Anita (*dances wildly about the stage*). Oh, he's coming, he's coming. I'm going to get to see Santa Claus! Is it not wonderful? I'm going to see him.

Let me look. (*Takes telescope.*) Oh, it's getting bigger
and *bigger* and bigger!

Sleigh bells heard outside at R., far away in the distance.

Jack Frost (*capering around*). Hurray! daddy's coming! daddy's coming!

Anita. Now I can hear the bells. Oh, it's coming closer
and *closer* and closer. Look out, it's going to hit the boat! (*Small toy air ship
flies across the stage at rear, with tiny lights twinkling in it. Stretch a wire
across rear of stage and high up, for the toy to run on.*)

Jack Frost. He flew right by us.

Anita. Maybe he didn't see the boat. Oh, now he isn't coming at all.

Jack Frost (*looking out at L.*). Yes, he is. He's landed right over there. Here
he comes; here he comes! (*Music and bells louder and louder.*)

Anita (*runs to L.*). Here we are, Santa Claus. This is the place. Come in.
Merry Christmas, Santa Claus, merry Christmas!

Loud fast music. Enter Santa Claus from L.

Santa Claus. Hello, there—where are you? It's so dark I can't see a single
thing.

Jack Frost. Hello, daddy; merry Christmas.

Santa Claus (*shaking hands with him*). Hello yourself. Merry Christmas to
you, too. Are you all ready for me?

Jack Frost. Yes, it's all ready. The magical tree is just waiting for your touch
to turn into a real Christmas tree.

Anita. Oh, we're going to have a real Christmas tree.

Santa Claus. Hello, who's this young person?

Jack Frost. This is Anita.

Santa Claus. And why isn't she sound asleep like the rest of the children?

Jack Frost. She's such a good little girl that I told her she could stay up with me and wait until you came.

Santa Claus (*laughs*). Oh, ho; so you've made a hit with my boy, Jack Frost, have you? Well, if that's the case, I guess you can stay.

Anita. But all of the children would like to see you, Santa Claus. See, they've prepared the candle and the wreath of holly and the star of Bethlehem all for you. There's Sergius and Tomasso and Hulda and Meeny and Hans and Yakob and Neelda and Ah Goo and Sano San and Mieze and the leetla Dutch twins, Klinker and Schwillie Willie Winkum. They've all been awfully good children. And Biddy Mary and Paddy Mike they brought the candle. They're good, too.

Santa Claus. Hurry, Jack, and fill up the shoes and stockings.

Jack Frost (*filling them from the sack*). Yes, daddy, I'm hurrying.

Santa Claus. It's just two minutes till Christmas morning. I've had a hard night's work and I think I'll just take a little vacation here in the steerage.

Anita. Oh, Santa Claus, may I wake up all the leetla children and let them see you?

Santa Claus. Yes, just as soon as you hear the chimes announcing the birth of Christmas Day.

Anita. And don't you have any other place to go this year?

Santa Claus. I hope not. Here I am in the middle of the ocean and my air ship is just about played out. Jack, dump everything out of the sack and we'll give the little immigrants the jolliest kind of a Christmas. I'm not going to lug all of those toys and candy and things back to the North Pole again.

Jack Frost (*empties sack on floor*). Here they are, daddy.

Santa Claus. Now, where's the tree?

Jack Frost (*goes to rear of the stage and removes the curtains that have been concealing the dazzling Christmas tree.*). There she is. Isn't she a beauty?

Anita. Oh, it's the greatest, most grand-a tree in all the world.

(*Faint chimes are heard in the distance.*)

Jack Frost. There are the chimes. It is Christmas Day. Merry Christmas, daddy; merry Christmas, Anita. Christmas Day is here.

Anita (*dancing around*). Merry Christmas, Jack Frost! Merry Christmas, Santa Claus! Merry Christmas, everybody! Merry Christmas to all the world. Wake up, Hulda! Wake up! (*Shakes her.*)

Jack Frost. Wake up, Paddy Mike and Sergius! Wake up! Merry Christmas!

Santa Claus. Wake up, Meeny and Biddy. It's Christmas morning. And you two little shavers, Klinker and Schwillie Willie Winkum, wake up and give Santa Claus a good, old hug!

(*The children all awaken. Rub eyes, stretch, etc.*)

Hulda. Oh, he's come, he's come, he's come! (*Runs and hugs* Santa Claus.)

Schwillie. Me, too. (*Hugs him.*) I said he'd come, didn't I, Klinker?

(*Lights all on full.*)

Klinker (*hugging* Santa Claus). Sure you did. And me, too, didn't I, Schwillie Willie Winkum?

Meeny. Oh, see the tree! The beautiful, beautiful Christmas tree.

Tomasso. And my leetla shoes are full of candy and toys.

Paddy Mike. Now, let's be all after giving three cheers for old Santa Claus. (*The cheers are given.*)

Anita (*bringing* Jack Frost *forward*). And this is the leetla Jolly Jack Frost.

Paddy Mike. Then three cheers for the leetla Jolly Jack Frost. (*The cheers are given.*)

Anita (*at C. with* Jack Frost). This was my Christmas secret. Santa Claus and the air ship and the Christmas tree and jolly Jack Frost and everything. This was the secret.

Paddy Mike. Now all of yeez give three cheers for Anita's secret. (*The cheers are given. Folk dance may be introduced. All sing Christmas carol as the curtain falls.*)

Curtain.

REMARKS ON THE PRODUCTION OF THE PLAY.

THE SCENERY.

The stage should be set to represent the steerage of a large ocean-going vessel. A good elaborate set may be arranged with very little expense by following the diagram. The back drop should be of light blue with a few cumulus clouds in white. The water line should be about one-fourth from the bottom, and from this line downward the scene should be darker blue, with white waves.

The background may be made from canvas or paper, as desired. A good effect has been produced by covering frames with tissue paper of the desired shades, the clouds and the water lines being cut from white paper and pasted on.

A railing runs across rear of stage. This railing is made of wood, with a tennis net serving for the wiring. Round life-savers are cut from paper, painted and attached to the railing. The ventilator and hatchways may be made from brown bristol board.

A large Christmas tree, lighted and decorated, stands at rear L. This is concealed by curtains.

A square box or table stands at rear C. Several barrels and boxes are at left front, and a box is at right front. A large barrel stands at left of center near the rear.

PROPERTIES.

Woolen stocking and knitting needles for Meeny.

Potatoes, knife, bowl for Biddy Mary.

Jack-stones for Sergius.

Tambourine for Anita.

Nickel (coin) for Jack Frost.

Violin for Tomasso.

White, lace-edged table cloth for Sergius.

Large candle decorated with red ribbons for Paddy Mike.

Bright picture of Virgin and Child for Tomasso.

Two large red stockings for Meeny.

Extra stockings for Yakob, Hans and Mieze.

Wreath of holly for Neelda.

Small wooden shoes for Tomasso.

Tinsel star for Hulda.

Telescope for Jack Frost. Made from a pasteboard roll covered with black cloth.

Toy air ship on a wire, to sail across stage at rear.
Pack of toys for Santa Claus.
Sleigh bells for Santa.
Chimes heard outside.

COSTUMES AND SUGGESTIONS.

Santa Claus—High boots. Red or brown coat or mackinaw, trimmed with fur (or cotton, dotted to imitate ermine fur). Cap to match coat. String of bells around neck. Pack of toys. White hair, mustache and long, white beard. Rosy cheeks. Do not wear a false-face, as this often frightens little children and makes the character seem unreal. When there are little children in the cast, their belief in Santa Claus must not be disturbed and the adult portraying the character need not attend the general rehearsals. The high boots may be shaped from black oil-cloth and drawn on over black shoes. Use a pillow or two to give an ample girth.

Jolly Jack Frost (aged 8 or 9)—A jolly, little chubby-faced boy who can memorize and deliver a long part. White stockings and shoes. Canton flannel suit of white, trimmed with long points cut from cloth, to represent icicles. Long-pointed cap of white, coming down around back of head and forming a long-pointed collar in front. The top point should be wired into position. Face and hands are powdered very white. Put small dabs of mucilage on the costume and sprinkle here and there with diamond dust powder. Trim the costume with bits of cotton to represent snow.

Anita (aged 8 or 9)—Dark hair and complexion. Black slippers with red rosettes or bows on them. White stockings. Green skirt. Small dark red apron, edged with white, black and green. Black spencer waist laced in front showing the white underwaist. Puffed sleeves falling to elbows. Green and red bows on elbows. Red silk handkerchief laid loosely over the shoulders. Gold beads around neck. Large earrings may be attached with court plaster. The headdress is a white oblong cloth, about six inches wide and about eighteen inches long. This cloth is gayly decorated with bands of red, green and black ribbons and the part on the head is padded with a small square of pasteboard. Tambourine decorated with red, black and green ribbons. A yellow silk handkerchief may replace the Sicilian headdress above described.

Hulda (aged 10)—A blonde girl with hair in two long braids. Wooden shoes, white stockings. Several very full underskirts. Long skirt of dark blue, made very full around the bottom. This skirt is patched with squares of dark red and striped goods. Large blue gingham apron edged with stripes of dark red. White waist. Blue bodice of same material as skirt. Small white cap fitting close to head in back, but turned back in front with points over each ear. Face round and rosy. If the wooden shoes are not easily obtained, fair substitutes may be made by covering an old pair of shoes with cream colored oil-cloth.

Sergius (aged 9)—Black oil-cloth leggings to knees. Dark trousers. Long Russian blouse of dark green coming nearly to knees and belted in at waist with black oil-cloth belt. Blouse edged with dark fur. Dark green cap trimmed with dark fur.

Meeny (aged 7)—Full white waist. Black bodice laced with red. Rather short red skirt, with black stripes sewed around bottom. White lace apron edged with red and black. White mob cap, puffed high in front. Red and black strings on cap which are tied under her chin. She carries a gray woolen sock, half finished, and knitting needles. Wooden shoes if possible.

Biddy Mary—Old shoes and ragged stockings. Old-fashioned dress, rather short, of plaid gingham. Worn gingham apron. Little square shawl of red and black checked goods, crossed on breast. Old-fashioned, little black bonnet tied under her chin. She carries a pan of potatoes and a knife. Her age is about 8.

Paddy Mike—Small boy of 7, dressed in a man's suit, cut down in a clumsy manner. Green vest.[Pg 89] Black swallow-tail coat. Little plug hat, made by covering a pasteboard form with black cloth. Shoes, old and worn, and many, many sizes too large for him.

Tomasso—Black slippers, white stockings. Red and yellow ribbons wound around legs. Black knee breeches and zouave jacket. Striped sport shirt. Red and yellow bows at knees and on shoulders. Red handkerchief knotted loosely at throat. Black felt hat, turned up side, gayly decorated with red and yellow ribbons. On his second entrance he carries a violin. A dark complexioned boy aged about 9.

The Dutch Twins (aged 4 or 5)—Hair in Buster Brown style. Very full blue trousers extending from under the arms to ankles. These are made of blue denim and patched with large vari-colored patches. Wooden shoes. Striped shirts. Dutch caps made of dark cloth, with a peak in front and a crown about six inches high. The twins should be dressed exactly alike and look as much alike as possible. Get chubby little fellows and thoroughly rehearse them in their part; in fact they must go over it so much that it must come as second nature to them on the night of the performance. Much of the humor in the play depends on the little Dutch twins. When they walk let them take long striding steps. Use frequent gestures, nods, etc., in their dialogue, but be sure and have every movement exactly the same at each rehearsal. These parts are not difficult if the little actors are well trained, and their success on the night of the performance will amply repay the trouble spent in their proper coaching.

Neelda—A little brunette girl, aged 4 or 5. Yellow sateen skirt and zouave jacket, trimmed with coarse black lace. Broad red sash tied on the side. White baby waist. Black lace mantilla over head, and hair dressed high with a high comb. Red rose over left ear.

Ah Goo—A chubby little Chinese boy of 5. White stockings, black slippers, white pajamas, slanting eyebrows, small round white cap and long pig-tail made of black yarn. Carries Chinese kite.

Yakob—Chubby boy of 6, dressed similar to twins, but in contrasting colors. Wears yarn stocking cap. Wooden shoes.

Hans—Tall, thin boy of 9. Dressed similar to the twins, but in brown. Tall black cap similar to those worn by the twins.

Mieze—Little girl of 3 or 4, dressed similar to Hulda, but in dark red and red and white checked gingham.

Sano San—Little Japanese girl in kimono and sash. Eyebrows slanting. Hair dressed high. Chrysanthemums over ears. Carries a paper parasol or fan.

The Christmas tree is for the whole school and is concealed during the first part of the play by curtains. If there is to be no tree, all reference to it may be omitted without injury to the continuity of the play.

Other songs may be substituted for the songs here given, but these have proved very successful in several performances of Anita's Secret.

CHRISTMAS WITH THE MULLIGAN'S

CHRISTMAS WITH THE MULLIGAN'S

A FUNNY CHRISTMAS PLAY IN THREE SHORT ACTS.

CHARACTERS

The Widow Mulligan   With a Heart Overflowing with Sunshine

Patsy   Aged Twelve

Matsy   Aged Eleven

Teddy Magee   Aged Seven

Nora Eudora   Aged Fourteen

Micky Machree   Aged Five

Bridget Honora   Aged Ten

Sweet Mary Ann   Aged Eight

Melissa   Aged Six

Clarissa   Aged Six

Wee Peter Pan   Aged Four

Mrs. O'Toole, A Neighbor   With a Heart Overflowing with Kindness

Time of Playing—*About One Hour.*

How they lived and what they wore will be told under the "Notes to the Manager" at the end of the play.

ARGUMENT.

Sure, there isn't much argument at all, at all. It's all happiness and merriment and love, and where there is happiness and merriment and love there isn't any time for argument. The Widow Mulligan is a cheerful washerwoman who lives in Mulligan Alley in Shantytown, surrounded by her ten little Mulligans, to say nothing of the goat, Shamus O'Brien. A good-hearted neighbor, Mrs. O'Toole, has a lively time with the goat, but she forgives all his misdeeds as it is Christmas Eve and the little Mulligans are starting out for a grand Christmas entertainment. When they return they entertain their mother and Mrs. O'Toole, and, incidentally, the audience.

But let's have done with the argument and let the fun begin.

Act I.

Scene: *The Mulligan's front room. Entrances at right and left. Window at rear. At rise of curtain* Mrs. Mulligan *is discovered at C., washing clothes in a tub.* Bridget Honora *and* Matsy *are hanging wet clothes on a line, which runs across the rear of the stage.*

Mrs. Mulligan (*singing to a made-up tune as she washes*).

Oh, give me a nice little home,
And plenty of suds in me tub,
And I will be happy all day,
With me rubby-dub, rubby-dub, dub.

The queen on her golden throne,
Will envy me here at me tub,
For no one's as jolly as I,
With me rubby-dub, rubby-dub, dub.

Sure, what would I do at a dance?
Or what would I do at a club?
But here in me kitchen I'm queen
With me rubby-dub, rubby-dub, dub.

Oh, give me a nice little home,
And plenty of suds in me tub,
And I will be happy all day,
With me rubby-dub, rubby-dub, dub!

Matsy. Maw, don't you think it's most time fer us to be going?

Mrs. Mulligan. Time to be going, is it? Well, I should hope not. Sure, half of the children are not dry yet, and the other half are not dressed. Bridget Honora, darlin', look in the other room and see how they're coming on. (*Exit* Bridget *at R.*)

Matsy. I think we ought to be there early, so as we can get a good seat on the front row. I don't want to miss nothing. (*Hangs up a boy's union suit.*)

Mrs. Mulligan. True for you, Matsy, and I don't want yeez to be missing anything either. It ain't like as if yeez go to a fine Christmas entertainment ivery night of yer lives. (*Washes.*)

Matsy. It's the first one any of us ever went to at all, at all. Do yeez think they be after having moving pictures?

Mrs. Mulligan. Of course not. Not in a Sunday School, Matsy. But belike they'll have a fine, grand Christmas tree with singin' and spaches and fine costumes and prisints for every one. (*Calls off R.*) Bridget Honora!

Bridget (*off R.*). Yes, maw?

Mrs. Mulligan. Come here.

Enter Bridget *from R.*

Bridget. Melissa and Micky Machree have been scrubbed until they shine. They're sitting in the window drying in the sun. Mary Ann is cleaning Peter Pan in the lard bucket, and Patsy is washing Teddy Magee in the rain-barrel. Nora is curling Clarissa's hair with the poker, and somebody's untied the goat.

Mrs. Mulligan. Untied the goat, is it? Matsy Mulligan, put on yer hat at once and see what's become of Shamus O'Brien. He's a good goat, is Shamus, but he's like the late Mr. Mulligan, he has a rovin' disposition and a tremenjous appetite. Hurry now, Matsy.

Matsy (*whining*). Aw, now, maw, I can't go and hunt the goat. I'm all dressed up for the entertainment. If I go after the goat, sure it's all mussed up I'll be.

Mrs. Mulligan. Yis, if I swat you one wid this wet cloth, it's worse than mussed up you'll be. Hurry after the goat. Niver a step does any Mulligan take from this house tonight until Shamus O'Brien is safe in the kitchen, wid his horns tied to the wash boiler.

Matsy. Sure, I dunno where to look fer him.

Mrs. Mulligan. Go over to Mrs. O'Toole's cabbage garden; like as not ye'll find him there. Sure, Shamus has a fine appetite for cabbages.

Matsy. Don't let 'em start afore I get back. I don't want to miss nothin'. (*Takes cap and exits L.*)

Mrs. Mulligan. Now, Bridget Honora, lave off hanging up the clothes and go in and see if Melissa and Micky Machree are dry yet. And if they are call me in and I'll attend to their costumes.

Bridget. Maw, Mary Ann's having an awful time. She's growed so that her skirt and her waist has parted company, and what she'll be after doing I don't know at all, at all.

Mrs. Mulligan. Is there anything she can use as a sash?

Bridget. No'm. Nora and Clarissa have used up all the sashes.

Mrs. Mulligan (*takes fringed bureau cover from wash-basket*). Look here, now, Bridget Honora, see what I've found in the wash. It's a tidy to go on top of a dresser, but I'm thinking it's just the thing to fill the gap between the skirt and the waist of Mary Ann.

Bridget. Yes, maw. (*Exit R.*)

Enter Patsy *from R. He runs in and is very much excited.*

Patsy. Oh, maw, maw, come quick! Hurry, or he'll be drowned.

Mrs. Mulligan. What is it, Patsy? Spake quick.

Patsy. It's Teddy Magee. I was givin' him a wash in the rain-barrel, when all of a sudden, bad luck to him, he slipped through me fingers and fell head-first down in the barrel. (*Cries.*) Oh, it's drownded dead he'll be. Oh, oh! (*Cries.*)

Mrs. Mulligan. Oh, me baby, me baby! (*Rushes out at R.*)

Enter Nora *and* Clarissa *from L.*

Nora. Now sit right down there, Clarissa, and don't be moving a hair, because you're all fixed and ready for the entertainment.

Clarissa. And how do I look, Nora?

Nora. Ye look like a Christmas angel, so you do. Your hair curled just lovely and your striped stockings will be the admiration and envy of the entire Sunday School.

Patsy. Oh, Nora Eudora, come on quick. Teddy Magee fell in the rain-barrel and it's drownded dead he is intirely. (*Cries.*)

Nora. In the rain-barrel? How did he get in the rain-barrel?

Patsy. Sure, I was washing him, I was. And he was that slippery with the soap that he slid through me fingers and down to the bottom of the barrel.

Nora. Oh, the poor little Teddy Magee. (*Runs out R., followed by* Patsy *and* Clarissa.)

Enter Mary Ann *and* Peter Pan *from L.*

Mary Ann. And how de yeez like me new sash, Peter Pan?

Peter Pan. Scwumptious.

Mary Ann. It's a tidy cover off'n a bureau, and I don't want to wear it at all, at all. Folks'll be after thinking I'm a bureau. Don't it look funny, Peter Pan?

Peter Pan. Scwumptious.

Mary Ann. I'm not going to wear it, so I'm not.

Enter Bridget *from L.*

Bridget. Mary Ann Mulligan, and what are yeez trying to do with your nice new sash?

Mary Ann. I ain't going to wear no tidy cover. Folks'll be after thinking I'm a bureau.

Bridget. Sure they'll think worse than that if yeez take it off. That's what comes of yer growing so fast. Yer skirt is fer six years old, and yer waist is fer six years old, and so you have to wear the sash to help out the other two years. Sashes are awful stylish, anyhow. It's pretty, too, ain't it, Peter Pan?

Peter Pan. Scwumptious.

Enter Mrs. Mulligan *from R., followed by* Pasty *and* Nora.

Mrs. Mulligan. It's lucky for him that there wasn't any more water in the rain-barrel, or he would have been drownded dead sure. Patsy, yeez had no business to let him drop. Nora, you go out and finish him. Where's Clarissa?

Enter Clarissa *from R.*

Clarissa. Here I am, maw.

Mrs. Mulligan (*looks her over carefully*). Well, you're all ready. That's one. Nora and Patsy and Matsy are all ready. That makes four. Mary Ann, are you all fixed?

Mary Ann. Yes, mum, but I don't like me sash at all, at all. Folks will all know it's a bureau tidy, it's got fringe and everything.

Mrs. Mulligan. Oh, ho, me fine young lady. I suppose yeez want a peek-a-boo dress all trimmed with mayonnaise ruffles down the bias, do you? It's lucky for you I found that tidy in the wash, so it is. And don't yeez eat too much or breathe hard or ye'll bust it, and then where'll you be at?

100

Bridget. Maw, Mary Ann's chewing her apron.

Mrs. Mulligan (*at the wash-tub*). Mary Ann Mulligan, take that apron out'n your mouth. I niver saw such a girl to be always chewing something. It's first yer dress and then yer apron or your petticoat, whatever happens to be your topmost garment. Clothes were not made to chew.

Enter Nora *with* Teddy, Melissa *and* Micky, *from L.*

Nora. Here they are, maw, all ready for the party.

Mrs. Mulligan. Are ye sure they're all clean?

Nora. I am that. They've been scrubbed until me two arms ache. And Micky's had a bath in the rain-barrel.

Micky. I have that, and I don't want another one, either.

Mrs. Mulligan. All yeez sit down and let me look ye over.

Nora. Have ye finished the washing, maw?

Mrs. Mulligan. For the prisint, yes. I have more important duties to perform. Now, first and foremost, don't walk pigeon-toed. Bridget, have ye got a clane handkerchief?

Bridget. Yis, mum.

Mrs. Mulligan. Well, don't forget to use it if the necessity arises, and you'd better set next to Peter Pan so's he can use it, too. He's been kinder nosey all day, and I shouldn't wonder if he wasn't coming down with a cold in his head. How do you feel, Peter Pan?

Peter Pan. Scwumptious.

Mrs. Mulligan. Micky Machree Mulligan, and what are yeez looking cross-eyed for? Do ye think it improves yer beauty?

Micky. I thought there was a speck of dirt on me nose.

Mrs. Mulligan. Well, there's not, and hold yer head up straight.

Patsy. Maw, ain't it most time to go?

Mrs. Mulligan. It lacks two hours yet of the time, and Matsy ain't come back with the goat. Whatever's become of Shamus O'Brien I'd like to know. Which of yeez seen him last?

Nora. I saw him this mornin'. He was eatin' a tin tomato can down in the alley.

Mrs. Mulligan. The poor thing! Now I suppose I'll have a sick goat on me hands on top of all me other troubles—and tomorrow's Christmas Day.

Bridget. Maw, suppose they won't let us in the Sunday School at all, at all. We don't belong to that Sunday School. What'll we do then?

Mrs. Mulligan. Indade they'll not turn yeez away on Christmas Eve. I chose that Sunday School for yeez to attend because it's the largest and the most fashionable in town. Mrs. Beverly Brewster goes there, and wherever Mrs. Beverly Brewster goes, sure yeez can count on it, it's bound to be most fashionable and select.

Mary Ann. But we never went there before. They'll think it's awfully nervy fer us to come buttin' in at their Christmas entertainment.

Mrs. Mulligan. Niver once will they. They'll welcome yeez with open arms and many Christmas prisints. And whatever yeez get be sure and say, "Thank yeez kindly and much obliged." Can ye do that?

All. Oh, yes, mum.

Mrs. Mulligan. Clarissa, look out'n the door and see if ye see anything of Matsy and the goat.

Clarissa. Yes, mum. (*Goes to door at L.*)

Mrs. Mulligan. Mary Ann Mulligan, quit fooling with yer sash. If I've told yer once I've told yer a hundred times it's liable to bust and yer skirt and yer waist ain't on speakin' terms.

Clarissa (*at door*). Maw, here comes Mrs. O'Toole.

Mrs. Mulligan. It's the goat. He's been filling himself up on the O'Toole cabbages. My, my, that goat'll be the death of me yet.

Enter Mrs. O'Toole, *limping in from L.*

Mrs. O'Toole. Good evening, Mrs. Mulligan.

Mrs. Mulligan. The same to ye, Mrs. O'Toole. Come in and set down.

Mrs. O'Toole. I have no time to set down, and I have no inclination to set down. And it's all on account of yer goat, Shamus O'Brien.

Mrs. Mulligan. Me goat, is it?

Mrs. O'Toole. It is the same, and it's an injured woman I am this night.

Mrs. Mulligan. My, my! I'll have to kill that old goat. He's entirely too obstreperous. And did he chase you, Mrs. O'Toole?

Mrs. O'Toole. Chase me? He did worse than chase me. He caught up with me.

Mrs. Mulligan. And where is he now?

Mrs. O'Toole. Niver a know do I know where he is. I left your boy Matsy chasing him down the alley with a rope.

Mrs. Mulligan. Bridget, go in the far room and get a wee drop of tay for Mrs. O'Toole.

Mrs. O'Toole. I can't drink any tay. I'm that injured I can't drink at all, at all.

Mrs. Mulligan. A drop of tay will warm ye up. Hurry, Bridget.

Bridget. Yis, mum. (*Exits R.*)

Mrs. O'Toole. I was out in me cabbage garden picking a bit of cabbage for me owld man's Christmas dinner. I was bending over looking at the cabbage whin all of a sudden I felt meself flying through the air and I landed in the watering trough, so I did. And it was full of water. And I'm almost killed entirely—and it's all the fault of your goat, Mrs. Mulligan.

Mrs. Mulligan. There, now, Kathleen, darlin', sit down and take things easy.

Mrs. O'Toole. I'll not sit down, Mollie Mulligan. Sure I'm thinking I'll be after spindin' the rist of me life standing up on me two fate.

Mrs. Mulligan. So the goat struck ye, did he?

Mrs. O'Toole. He did.

Mrs. Mulligan. My, my, the trouble I've had all along of that Shamus O'Brien. He's an awful goat, is Shamus O'Brien.

Enter Bridget *with two cups of tea.*

Bridget. Here's the tea, mum.

Mrs. Mulligan. Thank ye kindly, Bridget. Here, Kathleen, take a cup of tay and let it soothe your wounded feelings.

Mrs. O'Toole. Sure, it's more than me feelings that is wounded, Mrs. Mulligan. (*Drinks tea.*)

Clarissa. Maw, ain't it time we were starting for the entertainment?

Mrs. Mulligan. My, my, I've been that excited about the misdeeds of that rascal Shamus O'Brien that I had forgotten the Christmas entertainment entirely.

Mrs. O'Toole. Sure, your family looks as though they were going out in society, Mollie Mulligan.

Mrs. Mulligan. They are that. They're on their way to the fine church entertainment at the Sunday School down the strate.

Nora (*at door L.*). Maw, here comes Matsy with the goat. (*Looks out of door.*)

Mrs. Mulligan (*goes to door and speaks off L.*). Matsy Mulligan, tie that goat in the back yard and tie all his four fate together. I'll tach him a lesson, if it's the last thing I ever do. Patsy, go out and help your brother tie up Shamus O'Brien. (*Exit Patsy at L.*)

Mrs. O'Toole. Nora Eudora, darlin', have ye got a sofy pillow handy. I think if I had a couple of sofy pillows I could set down and enjoy me tay.

Nora. Yis, mum. Here's two of 'em. (*Arranges them in the chair.*)

Enter Patsy and Matsy from L.

Matsy. Come on, all of yeez, or we'll be late for the show. And I don't want to miss nothin'.

Mrs. Mulligan (*standing at R.*). I think yeez are all ready now. Let me see if there's anyone missing. (*Counting and pointing to each in turn.*)

There's Patsy and Matsy and Teddy Magee,
Nora Eudora and Micky Machree,
Bridget Honora and sweet Mary Ann,
Melissa, Clarissa and wee Peter Pan.

Patsy. We are all here, maw.

Mrs. Mulligan. Now, yer all ready. Throw out yer heads. Forward, march!

Children. Good-bye, maw.

Mrs. Mulligan. Good-bye, and the Lord love yeez all. Have a good time. Good-bye. (*The children march out at L.*)

Mrs. O'Toole. Ten of 'em. I don't see how ye ever manage to make both ends meet, Mollie Mulligan, with ten big, healthy children—to say nothing of the goat, Shamus O'Brien.

Mrs. Mulligan (*in door waving hand to children*). Good-bye. Have a good time. (*Yells.*) Mary Ann, don't let yer sash bust in two! (*Crosses to R. and sinks in chair.*)

Mrs. O'Toole. Ye have a fine family, Mrs. Mulligan. Ye have a fine bunch of boys, and ye have a bunch of girls, and ye have a fine bunch of babies; but ye have an awful goat.

Mrs. Mulligan. Shamus O'Brien is the pest of me heart, Kathleen O'Toole; so he is; but he's all that's left of me late husband's property. Michael Mulligan thought the world of that goat, he did.

Mrs. O'Toole. I'm a peaceful woman, Mollie Mulligan, and a calm, neighborly woman; but I don't like goats.

Mrs. Mulligan. I don't blame ye at all, at all, Kathleen. But poor Shamus O'Brien was probably only nosing around fer a bit of Christmas Eve dinner. I'll kape him tied in the future.

Mrs. O'Toole. Sure and it is Christmas Eve, isn't it?

Mrs. Mulligan. Indade it is, and for the sake of the holy eve, I think ye'd best be after forgiving the poor goat and not harbor any ill feeling agin him on Christmas Day.

Mrs. O'Toole. Harbor ill feeling, is it? Faith, then I'll not, Mollie Mulligan, and it's meself that'll be bringing over a big cabbage head on the morning for Shamus O'Brien's Christmas dinner.

Mrs. Mulligan (*rises*). I'll be after tidying up the house a bit. It's little enough I've got for the children's Christmas tomorrow morning; but at least I can have me house in order and a burning candle shining in the windy. (*Lights candle and sets it on table in front of the window.*)

This light shall burn on Christmas Day,
For Him who in the manger lay,
And all are welcome at my door,
The high, the low, the rich, the poor,
And every heart shall sing again
Of peace on earth, good will to men.

Mrs. O'Toole (*rises*). Your burning candle takes me back again to the days of me childhood in County Clare. Well do I mind me last Christmas Eve in ould Ireland, the little thatched cabin with its one window, the stinging smoke of the peat fire, the lads and the colleens and the ould piper—and the merry dances and songs, do ye remember, Mollie darling? (*Puts arms on hips, wags head from side to side and sings briskly:*)

1. Did you ev - er go in - to an I - rish-man's shanty, Where
2. Our nate lit - tle house, it looks out on the street, There's two
3. Sure the Mul - li-gans al-ways are hap-py and bright, They

mon - ey was scarce but where wel-come was plen-ty? A
beau - ti - ful rooms and a pig - sty com - plete. Each
sing in the morn-ing, they sing in the night, Now

three-leg - ged stool and a ta - ble to match it, But the
girl has a dress and each boy has a coat, There's
Pat - sy and Mat - sy are strong as can be, But the

door of the shan - ty is al - ways un-latched.
tin hap - py chil - dren, six pigs and a goat.
bil - ly - goat's strong-er than ath - er, you see!

Tee - oo - dle, dum-doo - dle, dum - doo - dle, dum day! Tee-

oo - dle, dum - doo - dle, dum - doo - dle, dum day! Tee-

oo - dle, dum-doo - dle, dum - doo - dle, dum day! Tee-

oo - dle, dum - doo - dle, dum-doo - dle, dum day!

Mrs. O'Toole (*sings briskly*):

Did you ever go into an Irishman's shanty,
Where money was scarce but where welcome was plenty?
A three-legged stool and a table to match it,
But the door of the shanty is always unlatched.
Tee-oodle, dum-doodle, dum-doodle, dum day!

(*Repeat until end.*)

Mrs. Mulligan (*faces her, assumes same position, sings briskly*):

Our nate little house, it looks out on the street,
There's two beautiful rooms and a pig-sty complete.
Each girl has a dress and each boy has a coat,
There's tin happy children, six pigs and a goat.
Tee-oodle, dum-doodle, dum-doodle, dum day!

(*Repeat until end.*)

Mrs. O'Toole (*sings*):

Sure the Mulligans always are happy and bright,
They sing in the morning, they sing in the night,
Now Patsy and Matsy are strong as can be,
But the billy-goat's stronger than ather, you see!
Tee-oodle, dum-doodle, dum-doodle, dum day!

(*Repeat until end.*)

Mrs. O'Toole *hums the song faster and begins to jig, by kicking out R. and
L. foot alternately, on first three lines and twirling on fourth line.*

At the beginning of the "Tee-oodle," Mrs. Mulligan *starts in and does
exactly as* Mrs. O'Toole *did on the first four lines, while* Mrs. O'Toole *skips
around stage in a circle.*

On the second verse they march forward and back, arms on hips. Forward again. Do-si-do (backs to back). March forward and back and then each twirls alone. Mrs. O'Toole *knocks over the table.* Mrs. Mulligan, *not to be outdone, knocks over the tub. The music becomes faster and faster.*

On third verse they jig alone, then forward and back, forward again and swing each other madly. While they are dancing they shout out occasionally, "Huroo for ould Ireland!" "That's me fine lady!" "Look at me now!" *etc.*

Curtain.

Act II.

Same as scene before. The wash-tub has been removed, also the washing from the line. The table has been straightened and Mrs. O'Toole *is seated there making a toy elephant.* Mrs. Mulligan *is seated at L. dressing a doll body in a baby's dress. The candle burns before the window.*

Mrs. O'Toole. It's lucky for us, darlin', that me husband is out at his lodge tonight. I can stay with you until the children return from the entertainment, and maybe it's a bit of a Christmas Eve high-jinks we can be having afterwards.

Mrs. Mulligan. Indade, I'm glad to have ye, Kathleen. Will your husband be long at lodge?

Mrs. O'Toole (*cutting the elephant's ears from brown paper*). He will that. Pat is the Grand Exalted Chafe Ruler of the Benevolent and Obstrep[Pg 111]erous Order of United Wooden-men, and he won't be home till marnin'.

Mrs. Mulligan. Is he now? The late Mr. Mulligan was niver much of a lodge joiner but that made no difference to him; he niver came home till marnin', lodge or no lodge.

Mrs. O'Toole. Remember, Mollie, you're coming over to dinner with us tomorrow. It's at one o'clock.

Mrs. Mulligan. Oh, Kathleen, I can't be laving the children at all, at all. On Christmas Day, too.

Mrs. O'Toole. Of course you can't. Ye're going to bring the children over with ye.

Mrs. Mulligan. The whole tin of them?

Mrs. O'Toole (*counting on fingers*).

Patsy and Matsy,

And Teddy Magee,
Nora Eudora,
And Micky Machree,
Bridget Honora,
And sweet Mary Ann,
Melissa, Clarissa,
And wee Peter Pan.

Mrs. Mulligan. And ye're willing for the whole bunch of us to come?

Mrs. O'Toole. All but the goat. I draw the line at Shamus O'Brien. Ye see it's this way. Me man, Pat, won a turkey in a raffle, and it's as big as a billy-goat. Then on top of that me daughter Toozy, that's married and lives in the country, sent us two chickens and a goose. And there's only me and Pat to ate all that.

Mrs. Mulligan. Kathleen O'Toole, it's a saint ye are.

Mrs. O'Toole. I says to Pat, says I, "Christmas ain't Christmas at all, at all, unless there's some children at the dinner." "What'll we do?" says Pat. "Invite the Mulligans," says I. And Pat was tickled to death. We've potatoes and squash and cabbage from me own garden, and we've oyster dressing and cramberries and stewed corn and apple fritters, and it's meself that has made eight mince pies, and four punkin ones—and I think we'll be after having a dinner on Christmas Day that would do credit to ould Saint Patrick himself.

Mrs. Mulligan. Sure, ye almost make me cry for joy, Kathleen O'Toole, and after the goat trated ye the way he did, too.

Mrs. O'Toole. If a woman can't be neighborly and loving on Christmas Day, Mollie Mulligan, sure I'm thinking she niver can be neighborly and loving at all, at all.

Mrs. Mulligan. And ye're aven makin' a bit of an iliphant for wee Peter Pan.

Mrs. O'Toole. I am that. Here's the little, fat body. (*Shows cylindrical piece of dark green squash.*) And here's the four legs. (*Shows two bananas cut in half.*) I'll just stick the legs on with nails—and there he stands. Now, here's a little potato for a head, and an ould skinny carrot for a trunk. I'll stick them on with a hair pin. (*Does so.*) Now, I'll stick on the ears and put in the shoe-button eyes, and with this wee bit of black paper for a tailpiece, and there ye are. Mr. Mumbo Jumbo Mulligan as natural as life and twice as handsome. (*Shows elephant to audience.*)

Mrs. Mulligan. Here's a doll baby I've dressed, but it's no head she has at all, at all.

Mrs. O'Toole. Use a big yellow apple or a wee yellow punkin, and put on a baby cap—and there ye are. Stick in some buttons for eyes, and a wee nose and mouth of red paper—and stick the head on the body with some hair pins, and the quane herself niver had a better doll baby.

Mrs. Mulligan. I'll put her right here on the table alongside of the iliphant.

Mrs. O'Toole. It's nine o'clock, it is. Isn't it time for the children to be home?

Mrs. Mulligan (*goes to door at R.*). It is that. (*Looks out.*) And here they come now.

(*The children are heard outside at R., singing to the tune of "Marching Through Georgia."*)

The Mulligans are coming now, as happy as can be,
We've been to the Sunday School and saw the Christmas tree,
Had a lark with Santa Claus and take a tip from me,
We'll all be marching on Christmas!

(*They march in from R., come down to front and line up.*)

Hurrah, hurrah, the Mulligans are here,
Hurrah, hurrah, for Santa Claus so dear,

Sure, it was a happy night,
The best one in the year,
And we'll be marching on Christmas!

Patsy got a trumpet, little Micky got a drum,
Matsy got a spinning top, you ought to hear it hum,
Clarissa got a candy cane, oh, won't we have the fun,
When we are marching on Christmas!

Hurrah, hurrah, the Mulligans are here,
Hurrah, hurrah, for Santa Claus so dear,
Sure, it was a happy night,
The best one in the year.
And we'll be marching on Christmas.

Nora got a picture-book, Melissa got a rake,
Every Mulligan on deck got oranges and cake,
Got a bag of candy, too—and got the stomachache,
But we'll be marching on Christmas.

Hurrah, hurrah, the Mulligans are here,
Hurrah, hurrah, for Santa Claus so dear,
Sure, it was a happy night,
The best one in the year.
And we'll be marching on Christmas.

(*They march around stage while singing the chorus, but line up in front while singing the verses. Use gestures to indicate the different persons and their toys.*)

Mrs. Mulligan. And did ye have a good time at the entertainment?

Bridget. Indade and we did that. It was as good as a circus parade and a picture show together. They treated us just lovely.

Mrs. Mulligan. Did they now? And you wasn't invited at all, at all.

Matsy. They gave us a seat way up in front, and Micky Machree acted like a pig, he did. Sure, he grabbed two oranges.

Mrs. Mulligan. Why, Micky, it's ashamed of ye I am.

Micky. I grabbed one to bring home to you, maw. I wanted you to have some of the Christmas present, too.

Mrs. Mulligan (*hugs him*). That's just like your father, Micky.

Mrs. O'Toole (*helping children off with hats, wraps, etc.*). And did ye have a good time, wee Peter Pan?

Peter Pan. Scwumptious, just scwumptious.

Mary Ann. And me sash niver busted in two at all. And I was one of the most stylish young ladies present, so I was.

Melissa. And they had a great, big Christmas tree. Clean up to the ceiling. With lights and toys and candy and little stars and bright fairies and angels and everything.

Patsy. And ould Santy Claus was there with a long white beard and a big pack of presents to everyone.

Clarissa. And I pulled Santa Claus' whiskers and they nearly fell off. He must be getting pretty old, 'cause his whiskers is coming loose.

Bridget. And Santy Claus called out all the names and everybody got up when their names was called and he gave 'em a present.

Micky. And they never called our names at all, at all.

Mrs. Mulligan. That's because they didn't know them. They didn't expect you at the party.

Mary Ann. It was a surprise party, maw.

Mrs. Mulligan. How was it a surprise party, Mary Ann?

Mary Ann. They all looked surprised when we came in.

Nora. When I saw they weren't going to call out our names, I just rose up in me seat and took the whole nine of 'em by the hand and marched right up to Santa Claus. He looked real surprised at the bunch of us.

Mrs. Mulligan. I should think he would.

Nora. "And who are you?" says he. "We're the ten little Mulligans from Mulligan Alley in Shantytown," says I, as cool as an icicle. "And we're ready for our presents, if it's all the same to you," says I. I thought they was going to fire us out, but what did he do but dive way down in the bottom of the sack and give every last one of us a present?

Teddy. And then he gave us bags of candy and oranges and apples and peanuts and popcorn and a candy cane, and then they had a show and Bridget Honora spoke a piece, she did.

Mrs. O'Toole. How did ye happen to spake a piece, Bridget Honora?

Bridget. I just stood up and told 'em I knowed one. There ain't nuthin' bashful about me. And I kind o' thought we ought to do something to help pay fer the good things they gave us.

Mrs. Mulligan (*petting her*). That's me good little Bridget Honora.

Melissa (*sees doll on table*). Oh, wee! Lookee there! Where'd she come from?

Mrs. O'Toole. Santa Claus was after being here while you were away and he left it for you.

Melissa. Is it all for me?

Mrs. Mulligan. It's the Mulligan dolly. It's fer all ten of yeez.

Patsy. She can have my share. I don't want no dolls.

Micky. Oh, look at the efulunt. Look at the efulunt.

Mrs. O'Toole. That is Mumbo Jumbo Mulligan from the sunny shores of Africa, way down in Louisiana.

Children. Who's he fur? Who's he fur?

Peter Pan (*takes elephant*). He's fur me. Scwumptious!

Teddy. Maw, they had a show there at the Sunday School. There was a wee little man, about so long (*measures about two feet*), and he stood up on a table and sang a song, so he did.

Patsy. Humph! I know how they did that. Matsy and me can show it to you.

Melissa. And they had the Turnover Topsy Turvies, too.

Clarissa. They stood upside down on their heads.

Mrs. Mulligan. My, my—but it must have been a wonderful show.

Mrs. O'Toole. Just think what we missed, Mollie Mulligan.

Matsy. I didn't miss nothin'. I never miss nothin' no time.

Nora. We could give just as good a show our own selves.

Others. Let's do it; let's do it. Let's give a show for maw and Mis' O'Toole.

Teddy. Would you like to see it, maw?

Mrs. Mulligan. If it ain't too late.

Mrs. O'Toole. What matters it how late it is? Christmas comes but once a year——

All. And when it comes it brings good cheer.

Mrs. Mulligan. Then sure we'll have the show. Poor folks can be just as happy on Christmas Day as rich folks. It's all in the way you feel about it.

Patsy. Now, maw, you and Mrs. O'Toole take your seats out there in front. (*Points to front row of the audience.*)

Matsy. I'll help you carry them out. (*They carry down two chairs from the stage and seat* Mrs. Mulligan *and* Mrs. O'Toole *in the audience.*)

Patsy. Now, we'll have to draw the curtain to get the stage ready.

Nora. And while we're getting ready Mary Ann can say her piece.

Curtain Falls.

Mrs. Mulligan (*in audience*). My, my, Kathleen, what a large crowd of people are here tonight. I'm afraid I'm not dressed up for the occasion.

Mrs. O'Toole. Dressed up, is it? Indade you are. Ye have on short sleeves and a low-neck dress. What more would ye want? There's the minister and his wife setting right back there. (*Speaks to them.*) Good avening, Brother ——; sure, it's a fine avening we're having, is it not?

Mrs. Mulligan (*speaks to a lady in audience*). My, my, is it yourself, Mrs. ——? Sure, I'm glad to see ye out. It's a long time since I've had the pleasure of seeing you. (*Speaks to several children.*) And there's —— and —— and ——. I'm glad to see all of yeez. Sure, some day yeez must come over to me house in Mulligan Alley and I'll let you play with the goat, Shamus O'Brien.

Mrs. O'Toole. I see the young ladies over there, and each one of them has a young man. My, my, it does me ould heart good to see the young folks enjoying themselves. It ain't so many years since me and Pat was courting each other just like the rest of yeez.

Mrs. Mulligan. Mrs. O'Toole, do you see that young man sitting there all by his lonesome? Ain't it a shame? And him such a good looking young feller, too. I've a good notion to go over there and cheer him up a bit. Maybe his girl is here with another fellow.

Mrs. O'Toole. Sure, there's plenty of girls here without any fellows at all, at all. Why should a young man sit all alone like a bump on a log, whin there's so many handsome colleens waiting for the chance at him?

Mrs. Mulligan. Whist, Mrs. O'Toole, it's making him embarrassed yeez are. Will you look at the red color in his face?

Mrs. O'Toole. If ye ask me my opinion, Mollie Mulligan, sure and I think he's after waiting fer one of yer own lovely daughters.

Mrs. Mulligan. Well, he might go further and fare worse. Nora Eudora's a fine girl, if I do say it myself.

Mrs. O'Toole. Whist, here comes Mary Ann out in front of the curtain to spake her piece.

(Mary Ann *comes in front of the curtain, makes a bow and recites:*)

LETTER TO SANTA CLAUS

Blessed old Santa Claus, king of delights,
What are you doing these long winter nights?
Filling your budgets with trinkets and toys,
Wonderful gifts for the girls and the boys.
While you are planning for everything nice,
Pray let me give you a bit of advice.

Don't take it hard if I say in your ear,
Santa, I thought you were partial last year;
Loading the rich folks with everything gay,
Snubbing the poor ones who came in your way.
Now of all times of the year I am sure
This is the time to remember the poor.

Plenty of children there are in our city,
Who have no fathers or mothers to pity;
Plenty of people whose working and heeding
Scarcely can keep all their dear ones from needing.
Now, if I came every year in December,
These are the ones I would surely remember.

Once on a beautiful Christmas you know
Jesus our Saviour was born here below,
Patiently stooping to hunger and pain,
So He might save us, His lost ones, from shame;
Now if we love Him, He bids us to feed
All His poor brothers and sisters who need.

Blessed old Nick! I was sure if you knew it,
You would remember and certainly do it;
This year, at least, when you empty your pack,

Pray give a portion to all who may lack.
Then, if there's anything left and you can
Bring a small gift to wee Peter Pan.
—*Emily H. Miller.—Adapted.*

Mrs. O'Toole (*applauding vigorously*). Wasn't that dandy? Sure, little Mary Ann has a wonderful education, so she has!

Mrs. Mulligan. She takes after her own mother. I was just like her when I was that age.

Mrs. O'Toole. And you're just like her still, Mollie Mulligan. Sure you're the sunshine of Mulligan Alley and the belle of Shantytown.

Mrs. Mulligan. Whist now! It's covered I am wid blushes. But, hush! I think the show is about to begin.

Act III.

Curtain rises disclosing the same scene. Three long sheets hang on the line, reaching down to the floor and extending clear across the stage. The children are behind the sheets. The line is about three and one-half feet high. The table sets obliquely in front of the door at R. It is covered with a sheet or long cloth reaching to the ground. Patsy *and* Teddy *form the dwarf.*Patsy, *coatless, has a long pair of striped stockings on over his arms, and a pair of shoes on his hands, ornamented on insteps with large rosettes.* Teddy *stands behind him and thrusts his arms as far as they will go under* Patsy's *armpits. A kind of a tunic covers both. Wear a large crimped frill or an enormous turned-down collar.*

Patsy *stands behind table and places his shoe-clad hands upon it, which represent the feet of the dwarf. The door curtains are fastened together a few inches above his head, concealing*Teddy.

Patsy *must lean slightly over the table or the legs will not appear to support the body.*

When the curtain is up, enter Matsy *from L. dressed as a Showman.*

Matsy (*bows to audience, speaks in a loud voice, using megaphone*).

Come and see Jumbo, Samson symbolical!
Come and see Slivers, Clown really comical!
Come and see Zip, the foremost of freaks!
Come and see Palestine's Sinister Sheiks!
Eager Equestriennes, each unexcelled,
Most mammoth menagerie ever beheld,
The Giant, the Fat Girl, the Lion-faced Man,
Aerial Artists from far-off Japan,
Audacious Acrobats shot from a gun,
Don't miss the greatest show under the sun!

Now, if you will kindly lend me your ears for a moment, I will fill them free of charge with a few words concerning the world's greatest assortment of marvelous monstrosities. In the first cell we have Senor Macaroni Spaghetti from the land of the banana. The senor is thirty-nine inches high, and, strangely enough, thirty-nine years old, to say nothing of the fact that he weighs thirty-nine pounds. (Patsy *scratches his nose with his foot.*) He arrived last week by parcel post to join our circus. The senor is looking for a wife. Oh, you needn't laugh! It's true. Some of you near-sighted ladies should have brought magnifying glasses, for Senor Macaroni Spaghetti is the smallest speck of humanity that ever lived in captivity. He stands on a silver dollar and puts his hand in a thimble. (Teddy *makes funny gestures during this entire speech.*) The senor will now entertain you in his entertaining way.

Patsy (*sings*).

SPAGHETTI FROM OLD ITALY.

Me name is Spaghetti, I came o'er the sea,
To visit this land from old Italy,
I have a small monkey, he jumps with a string,
And if he was here to you he would sing:
(*Dances.*) Tee-oodle, dum-doodle, dum-doodle, dum day!

(*Repeat until end.*)

I once fell in love with the sweet Antoinette,
She say she will marry the little Spaghett,
But she said she no like-a a hand-organ man,
So I stand on the corner and sell-a banan.
(*Dances.*) Tee-oodle, dum-doodle, dum-doodle, dum day!

(*Repeat until end.*)

I wed Antoinetta and live in a flat,
I buy-a fine clothes and a big silk-a hat,
I make-a much money and this little gent,
He maybe some day will be big President.
(*Dances.*) Tee-oodle, dum-doodle, dum-doodle, dum day!

(*Repeat until end.*)

Matsy. And now, ladies and gentlemen, I'll call your attention to the seven
little Sunbonnet babies. Behold them, them famous Mulligan twins. (*Exits
L.*)

125

The heads of Nora, Micky, Bridget, Mary
Ann, Melissa, Clarissa *and* Peter *appear above the sheets at rear. Each
wears a large sunbonnet. They sing to the tune "Tramp, Tramp, Tramp!"*

Little Mulligans are we, and our hearts are light and free,
For it's Christmas Eve and soon we'll be in bed,
We're peculiar little folks, full of jollity and jokes,
And you ought to see us stand upon our head!

Tramp, tramp, tramp, we'll soon be marching,
We are going off to bed,
But before we leave you now,
Each of us will show you how
Little Mulligan can stand upon her head.

*(All disappear under sheet. They repeat chorus and hold up their arms
above the sheet. The arms are covered with stockings and shoes are on their
hands. They slap hands together, making feet dance, etc.)*

Tramp, tramp, tramp, we'll soon be marching,
We are going off to bed,
But before we leave you now,
Each of us will show you how
Little Mulligan can stand upon her head.

(Repeat.)

Mrs. Mulligan (*from audience*). Nora! Bridget! Mary Ann! What do ye
mane! You'll kill yourselves entirely. (*Rushes to the stage, followed by* Mrs.
O'Toole.) If you stand on your head like that, all your brains will rush down
into your fate.

Nora (*head above curtain*). That's the way they did in the show. (*All come
out on stage.*)

Mrs. O'Toole. Well, well, well, wonders will never cease. Sure, I niver spint such a fine Christmas Eve in all me life before.

Mrs. Mulligan (*stands C. facing audience, surrounded by the ten children.*) Sure, I think we've had a fine Christmas celebration, don't you? And before ye go let this sink down deep in your hearts and minds—it doesn't take money and fine clothes and costly gifts to make a fine Christmas at all, at all. All it takes is loving hearts and loving hands, and merry faces of happy boys and girls. We didn't have any money—but you see what a lovely time we've had—and it's all because the spirit of Christmas was in our hearts— and the spirit of Christmas means love, and love is the greatest thing in all the world. Merry Christmas to all of yeez, and may ye never regret the time you spent Christmas Eve with the ten little Mulligans.

Curtain.

NOTES TO THE MANAGER.

WHERE THE MULLIGANS LIVED.

The scenery is very simple or may be dispensed with entirely. Entrances R. and L. and a window at the rear are necessary. An old table stands in front of the window, and a larger table, also old, stands down R. Several soap boxes are down L. and these with an upturned bucket serve as seats for the Mulligans.

An old rag carpet covers the floor. A wash-tub, with wash-board, clothes, etc., stand at C. Two rickety chairs are on the stage, one R.C. and one L.C., the latter a rocking-chair. The larger table is covered with a well worn red cloth and supports an old-fashioned lighted lamp.

Several tin cans, filled with bright flowers, stand on the table in front of the window. Curtains or bed comforts are draped over the door at R. An old sofa stands up L. Colored prints adorn the walls.

A clothes line runs across the stage at rear. On this line several garments are drying, bright stockings, a union suit, red flannels, etc. Remember the scene is laid in Mulligan Alley and the stage must be arranged according to Mulligan taste.

WHAT THE MULLIGANS WORE.

Mrs. Mulligan—Powdered hair, parted in middle and combed over ears, somewhat unkempt. Well worn, old-fashioned cloth waist, with sleeves rolled up and open in the neck. Skirt of contrasting color. The skirt is turned up, showing flannel petticoat. Unstarched and rather soiled dark gingham apron, of ample proportions, but without bib. Hair twisted in knob at the back of head. Large, old shoes.

Matsy and Patsy—Long, tattered trousers, old suspenders, large, well worn shoes, calico shirts, torn and patched. Bright calico neckties. Caps. In Act III Matsy wears a large black mustache, a long black coat, much too large, and a stiff hat three sizes too big, while Patsy wears the dwarf's tunic and has his face made up yellow, with rouge on cheeks.

Teddy and Micky—Short trousers, well worn and patched. Striped stockings. Old shirts.

Nora and Bridget—Ankle skirts, waists of a different color. Bright calico bows. Large hair ribbons.

Mary Ann, Melissa and Clarissa—Short skirts. Striped stockings. Old shoes. Funny hats and waists.

Peter Pan—Calico slip. Baby's hat.

Mrs. O'Toole—Old-fashioned walking dress of bright colors. Shawl and little bonnet. Red wig, if desired.

THE WISHING MAN

THE WISHING MAN

A CHRISTMAS WHIMSY FOR SWEETE CHARITIE.

IN THREE SHORT ACTS.

As presented by Class No. 10, Wesley Chapel, Columbus, Ohio. Re-written from memory.

CHARACTERS.

The Wishing Man

The Roly-Poly Dumpling

The Attenuated Tootsy

The Enlarged Snookums

Grandpa Green

Grandma Green

Father Fritz

Mother Fritz

Nurse Maid

Dumpling

Tootsy

Snookums

Ka-zin-ski

Teddy Bear

Jimmie Bear

Baby Jumbo

Annette

Babette

Olivette

Private Black

Private Jack

Private Mack

Jim Dandy, *a Stick of Candy*

Time of Playing—*About Forty-five Minutes.*

For description of costumes, scenery, etc., see "Remarks on Production" at the end of the play.

Act I.

Scene: *A room in* Father Fritz's *house. Doors at R. and L. Small table down L. with three chairs around it. Sofa down R. Easy chair down C. Lighted lamp on table. Window at rear.*Dumpling *is seated on a rocking-horse at rear C.* Grandpa *stands by him helping him rock it.* Tootsy *is on a rocking-horse at L. front, with* Father *and* Mother *helping her rock it.* Snookums *is on a baby rocking-horse at R. front, with* Grandma *and* Nurse Maid *in attendance. Very little furniture on stage. If the rocking-horses are not easy to get,* Dumpling *and* Tootsy *may be astride of sticks with horses' heads.*

Curtain rises to bright music.

All (*sing*).

HOP, HOP, HOP!

1. Hop, hop, hop! Nim-ble as a top, Where 'tis smooth and
2. Whoa, whoa, whoa! How like fun you go! Ver-y well, my
3. Here, here, here! Yes, my po-ny dear; Now with oats and

where 'tis sto-ny, Trudge a-long, my lit-tle po-ny,
lit - tle po-ny, Safe's our jaunt tho' rough and sto-ny,
hay I'll treat you, And with smiles will ev-er greet you,

Hop, hop, hop, hop, hop! Nim-ble as a top.

Spare, spare, spare, spare, spare! Sure e-nough we're there.

Po - ny, po - ny dear! Yes, my po - ny dear.

Dumpling (*dismounting*). Whoa, there, Jimmie! Oh, Grandpa, I do love my pony. It's the best of all my presents.

Grandpa. Well, it's time you put him in his stall.

Tootsy (*dismounting*). I'm going to call my pony after Mr. ——. (*Insert the name of some well known man.*) 'Cause he looks just like him.

Grandma (*helping* Snookums *from pony*). And what are you going to call your pony, Snookums?

Snookums. Going to call him Elizabeth, after you, Grandma.

Grandma (*kisses her*). That's my baby!

Mother. Grandma, we'd better get our hats and coats. It's nearly time for the car to be after us.

Father. Come, Grandpa. It's nearly eight o'clock.

Grandpa. But I don't like to leave the children.

Dumpling. And we don't like to have you leave us, either. My, this has been the grandest Christmas day I've ever seen.

Mother. Come, Grandma. (*Exits L. with* Grandma.)

Grandpa. Come, children. (*They gather around him.*) I'm glad you've had such a happy Christmas. You got everything you wanted, didn't you?

Tootsy. Yes, everything. My, I wish Christmas would come every day.

Dumpling. Tell us the story about old Saint Nick, Grandpa.

Grandpa. Do you want to hear that old chestnut again?

Children. Oh, yes, yes!

Grandpa (*takes* Snookums *on his lap, the other children stand by his knee.*)

'Twas the night before Christmas, when all through the house
Not a creature was stirring, not even a mouse;
The stockings were hung by the chimney with care,
In hopes that Saint Nicholas soon would be there.
The children were nestled all snug in their beds,
While visions of sugar-plums danced through their heads;
Grandma in her kerchief and I in my cap,
Had just settled our brains for a long winter's nap,—
When out on the lawn there arose such a clatter,
I sprang from my bed to see what was the matter.
Away to the window I flew like a flash,
Tore open the shutters and threw up the sash.

When what to my wondering eyes would appear
But a wee little sleigh and eight little reindeer,

With a wee little driver, so lively and quick,
I knew in a moment it must be Saint Nick.
More rapid than eagles his reindeers they came,
And he whistled and shouted and called them by name:
"Now, Dasher! Now, Dancer! Now, Prancer and Vixen!
On, Comet! On, Cupid! On, Donder and Blitzen!
To the top of the porch, to the top of the wall!
Now, dash away, dash away, dash away, all."

So up to the housetop the reindeer they flew,
With a sleigh full of toys, and Saint Nicholas, too.
As I drew in my head and was turning around,
Down the chimney Saint Nicholas came with a bound.
He was dressed all in red from his head to his foot,
And his clothes were all tarnished with ashes and soot.
His eyes, how they twinkled! His dimples how merry!
His cheeks were like roses, his nose like a cherry.
He had a broad face and a little round belly
That shook when he laughed, like a bowl full of jelly.

A wink of his eye and a twist of his head
Soon gave me to know I had nothing to dread.
He spoke not a word, but went straight to his work
And filled all the stockings; then turned with a jerk,
And laying his finger aside of his nose,
And giving a nod, up the chimney he rose.
He sprang to his sleigh, to his team gave a whistle,
And away they all flew like the down of a thistle;
But I heard him exclaim e'er he drove out of sight:
"Happy Christmas to all, and to all a good-night!"
—*Clement C. Moore.*

Children. Oh, that was just lovely.

Tootsy. I just wish I could see him. Just once!

Dumpling. And so do I. I'm going to catch him some Christmas Eve.

Snookums. Me, too!

Enter from L., Mother *and* Grandma, *wearing winter coats and hats. They carry coats and hats for* Father *and* Grandpa.

Mother. Here, Grandpa, put on your coat and hat, or we'll be late for the dinner. (*Helps him.*)

Grandpa. I'd rather stay here and talk to the children.

Father (*putting on his coat*). But Aunt Clara is expecting us.

Grandma. And the auto is at the door.

Grandpa. Dumpling, are you sure you got everything you wanted for Christmas?

Dumpling. I can't think of anything else.

Grandpa. If you didn't, and if all three of you children can agree on anything else, it shall be yours if money can buy it.

Tootsy. Money can buy everything, can't it, Grandpa?

Grandpa. No, my dear, not quite everything.

Dumpling. But suppose we wish for something that money can't buy?

Grandpa. I'd try to get it for you some other way.

Tootsy. How, Grandpa; how?

Grandpa. Why, I'd tell the Wishing Man. He'd get it for you.

Grandma. Come along, John; don't put such nonsense in the children's heads.

Father. We must hurry along to Aunt Clara's, children. But this is Christmas night. You may all stay up tonight just as long as you wish.

Dumpling. Oh, can we? Can we?

Mother. Yes. Cecelia will look after you. Cecelia?

Nurse Maid. Of course I will, mum.

Mother. Come along, now. We must hurry. (*Kisses the children and goes out R. with* Grandma, Grandpa *and* Father.)

Tootsy (*dancing around*). Oh, we can stay up just as long as we wish! Goody, goody! Why that is the very best gift of all.

Nurse Maid. Now you children be good, and if you want me, call out. I'll be down in the kitchen with the cook. (*Goes out at L.*)

Dumpling. Now we're left all alone.

Tootsy. I don't see why Aunt Clara couldn't have invited us to her dinner party, too.

Snookums (*playing with doll*). Snookums likes dinner party.

Dumpling. It's 'cause we ain't big enough.

Tootsy. My, I wisht I was a great, great, great big girl.

Dumpling. There, that's a wish that money can't buy.

Tootsy. Grandpa said he'd get us anything we wished for.

Dumpling. What do you wish, Snookums?

Snookums. Wish Grandpaw would come home.

Tootsy. I know a real good wish. I wish it were Christmas every day. Don't you, Dumpling?

Dumpling. No, I don't. We'd have to have a present and a tree and a turkey and plum pudding every day of our lives. We'd get awfully tired of it after a while. Just think, we'd have to give away about a million presents every year.

Tootsy. I'll tell you what I really do wish.

Dumpling. What?

Tootsy. I wish we could do just like grown up folks do. I wish I was the biggest little girl in all the world.

Dumpling. And I wish so, too. I wish we were just awfully, awfully, awfully big—and then we could go to Aunt Clara's dinner party, and everywhere.

Snookums. Me wish me was great big Snookums.

Tootsy. But money couldn't buy that wish, Dumpling.

Dumpling. No, that's right. But Grandpa said if he couldn't buy our wish he'd get it some other way.

Tootsy. How could he get it?

Dumpling. He said he'd tell the Wishing Man.

Tootsy. My, I wonder if there really is such a person!

Dumpling. I don't know. But I'd like to see him if there is.

Tootsy. I'll make a rhyme.

Good Mr. Wishing Man, how do you do?
If there is such a person, we'd like to see you!

Dumpling.

If you come from afar, if you come from near,
Good Mr. Wishing Man, appear, appear!

The Wishing Man *rolls out from under the table, rises, faces the three
children, arms akimbo.*

Wishing Man (*after a pause, drawls*). Well?

Dumpling *and* Tootsy (*frightened, down R.*). Well? (*They look at each
other, pause, then repeat.*) Well!

Snookums (*comes in front of them, stands facing the* Wishing Man, *arms
akimbo*). Well?

Wishing Man. Well, I'm here.

Dumpling. Who's here?

Wishing Man. Why, *I* am here. You said you would like to see me and so I
have come. *I'm* here.

Tootsy. Are you the Wishing Man?

Wishing Man. That's my name. (*Sings to the tune of "Wearing of the
Green." He sings briskly, shaking head in time and dancing a step or two.*)

I'm the friend of all the children,
And I'll help you if I can,
Just tell me what your wishes are,
For I'm the Wishing Man.
I have wishbones on my fingers,
I have myst'ry in my eyes,
My clothes are trimmed with horseshoes,
And they're stained with magic dyes.
My pocket's full of rabbits' feet,
And clover leaves and charms,

For luck I've got a big black cat
All tattooed on my arms,
I'm a friend of all the children,
And I'll help you if I can,
So tell me what your wishes are—
For I'm the Wishing Man.

I come from a distant country
Away up near the pole,
But the things that I am telling you,
You mustn't tell a soul.
I know every witch and goblin,
And if you would believe!
I have fortunes in my pocket-book,
And wonders up my sleeve.
When any little boy or girl
Says, "Wishing Man, appear!"
I jump right up from underneath,
And here I am, my dear!
I'm a friend of all the children,
And I'll help you if I can,
So tell me what your wishes are—
For I'm the Wishing Man.

Dumpling. And can you really grant us anything we wish for?

Wishing Man. I can, if it's a good wish—and if you all agree on the same thing.

Tootsy. Anything in the wide, wide world?

Wishing Man. Well, pretty nearly anything. Would you like some new toys?

Tootsy. Oh, no, thank you. This is Christmas, you know, and we got ever so many toys.

Snookums. Ever so many toys.

Wishing Man. I don't see what you called me for. You seem to have everything you want.

Dumpling. Oh, no, we haven't. We've made a wish, and we're all agreed on it.

Wishing Man. Are you sure it's a good wish?

Dumpling. Oh, yes, it's an awful good wish. You see, we want to be great big children so we can stay up late at night and go to Aunt Clara's dinner parties. That's our wish. We want to be the biggest children there are anywhere.

Wishing Man (*laughs heartily*). Oh, ho, ho, ho! That's the funniest wish I ever heard since I've been in the wishing business. So you want to be the very biggest children there are anywhere, do you?

Tootsy. Yes, sir; that's just what we want. I want to be a great, big, tall little girl.

Wishing Man (*laughing*). A great, big tall little girl, hey?

Dumpling. And I want to be a great, big, big, *big* little boy.

Wishing Man. Oh, a big, *big*, big little boy, hey?

Snookums. And so do I.

Wishing Man. And so do you, hey?

Children. Yes, sir; that is our wish.

Wishing Man. Well, I'll have to see if I can accommodate you. It's a pretty big job, you know.

Tootsy. You said you could give us anything we wished for.

Wishing Man. But I didn't think you'd wish for anything like that.

Dumpling. That's the only thing we want, Mr Wishing Man.

Wishing Man (*rubbing his chin and speaking thoughtfully*). Well, now—let me see. I'm afraid it's too big a job for me. In the first place I haven't any marble.

Children. Marble?

Wishing Man. Yes. In order to make you grow and grow and grow, you'll have to stand on marble.

Tootsy. We have a marble-top table in the front hall.

Dumpling. Oh, yes. And we can all stand on top of the table.

Wishing Man. But I have to stand here by the open window.

Tootsy. Well, we can go in there and leave the door open. You can stay here and make our wish come true. Come on, Dumpling.

Wishing Man. Wait a minute, wait a minute. Are you all of you sure you want to be made into great big, big little children?

Children. Yes, all of us.

Wishing Man. All right. If that's your wish, it's no business of mine. Go out in the front hall and climb on the marble-top table and I'll see what I can do for you.

Tootsy. Oh, come on, quick, Dumpling, before he changes his mind. (*Runs out R. with* Dumpling *and* Snookums, *the latter taking very long strides.*)

Wishing Man. It's a very foolish wish, but maybe they'll be satisfied if I make them the biggest children on earth. (*Throws back curtains at the window.*) I'll see what I can do.

Dumpling (*outside*). I'm standing up on the table now.

Wishing Man.

Hickety, kickety, setting sun,
(*Making mysterious passes.*)
Thunder, lightning, flash of a gun!
Let him grow bigger, it won't be much fun;
Hickety, kickety, number one!

(*Lights flash out, then on again, then out. Low rumbles of thunder heard. Lights on again, then off. Loud crash outside.*)

Tootsy. Now it's my turn. I'm on the table.

Wishing Man.

Witchery, twitchery, kangaroo,
Thunder and lightning, Kalamazoo!
Lengthen her, strengthen her, rip, bazoo,
Make her a giantess, number two!

(*Lightning and thunder as before.*)

Snookums (*outside*). Now, Mr. Wishing Man, I'm on the table.

Wishing Man. That's the Baby Snookums. Very well, little Snookie Ookums! I'll change you into the biggest baby on earth.

Rumpety, thumpety, Kankakee,
Lengthen him out to six foot three!
The biggest baby we ever did see,

Rumpety, thumpety, number three!

(*Same noises as before, only louder.*)

Enter Nurse Maid *from L.*

Nurse Maid. Goodness, gracious! Is it a tornado or an earthquake? (*Sees* Wishing Man.) Oh! (*Screams loudly.*) And who are you? Murder! Thieves! Robbers! Where's me children? Where's little Dumpling and Tootsy and Baby Snookums? (*Fast, loud music.*)

Wishing Man (*yells*). Where are your children?

Enter Big Dumpling, Big Tootsy *and* Big Snookums. *They join hands and dance around at R.*

Wishing Man. There they are. There are little Dumpling and Tootsy and Baby Snookums.

(Nurse Maid *looks at children, screams loudly, throws up her arms and faints in a chair at L. of stage.* Wishing Man *stands at C. with arms akimbo, laughing at her. The three big children dance in a circle at R.*)

Curtain.

Act II.

Scene: *No scene at all. The action takes place in front of the closed curtains. Note: During this act the managers should be arranging the stage for the next act.*

The children who are present in the audience should be given seats down in front. At this point they rise and go upon the stage in front of the curtain and sing, accompanied by a chorus of older children behind the scenes. An adult leader may appear with the children. All sing, marching around platform and acting out the song:

FOLLOW ME, FULL OF GLEE.

Movement Song.

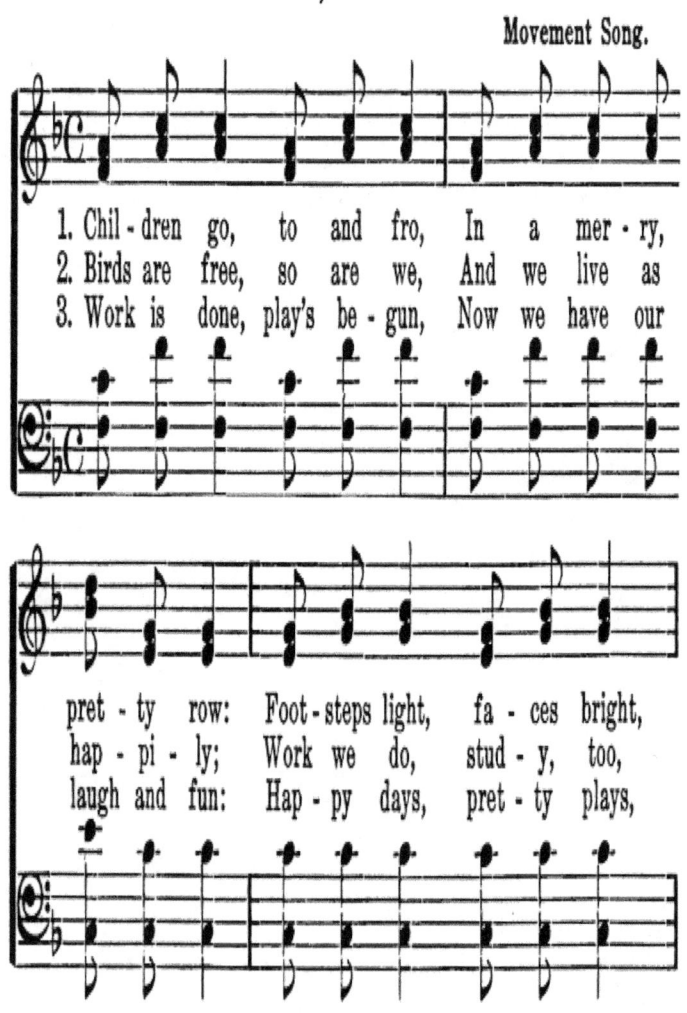

1. Chil - dren go, to and fro, In a mer - ry,
2. Birds are free, so are we, And we live as
3. Work is done, play's be - gun, Now we have our

pret - ty row: Foot - steps light, fa - ces bright,
hap - pi - ly; Work we do, stud - y, too,
laugh and fun: Hap - py days, pret - ty plays,

'Tis a hap-py, hap-py sight; Swift-ly turn-ing
Learn-ing dai-ly some-thing new; Then we laugh, and
And no naught-y, naught-y ways. Hold-ing fast each

round and round.* Do not look up-on the ground,
dance, and sing, Gay as birds or an-y-thing:
oth-er's hand, We're a hap-py, cheer-ful band;

Fol-low me, full of glee, Sing-ing mer-ri-ly.

CHORUS.

Sing-ing mer-ri-ly, mer-ri-ly, mer-ri-ly,

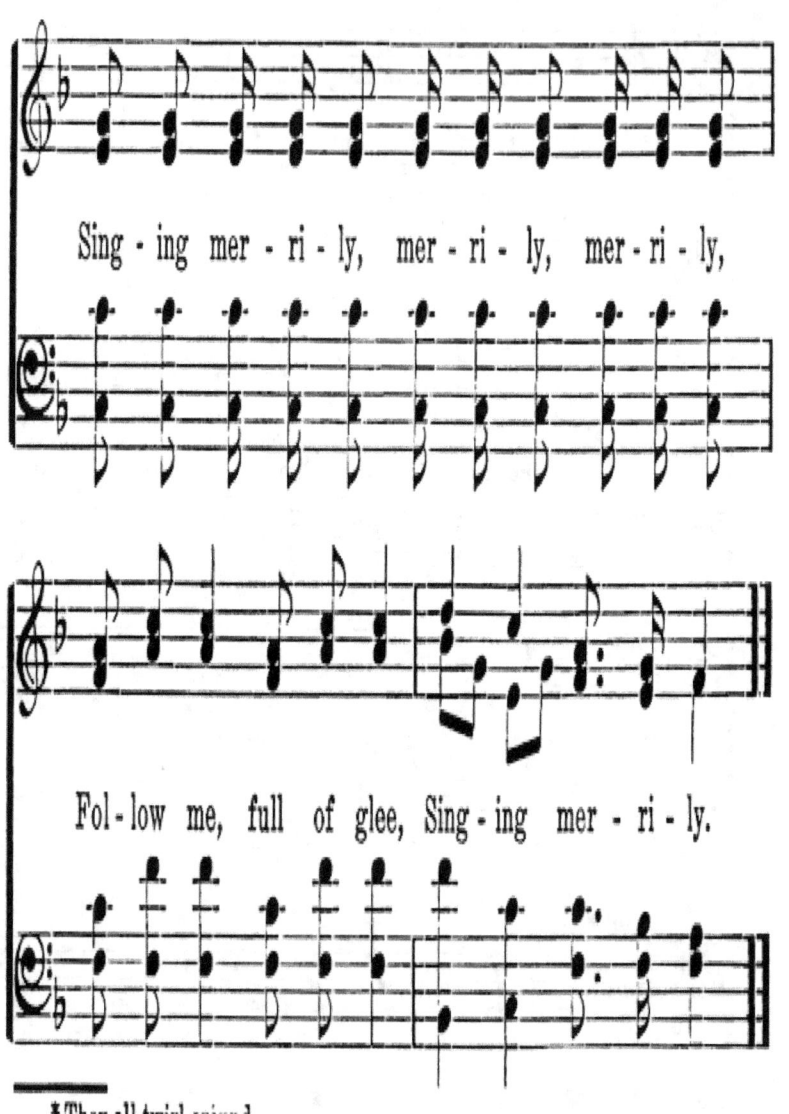

Sing - ing mer - ri - ly, mer - ri - ly, mer - ri - ly,

Fol - low me, full of glee, Sing - ing mer - ri - ly.

* They all twirl around.

(The music continues softly as they resume their seats in the audience. After a pause the Wishing Man *sticks his head out from the curtains. He takes one step in front, bows, then skips down to front and bows again.)*

Wishing Man. Hello, little boys and girls, how do you do this fine winter night? I know what each of you has been thinking. You've been wishing that *you* could meet the Wishing Man and that he would make *your* wishes come true. Now, haven't you? Well, I've made that wish come true. You wished to meet me, and here I am. I've been watching you all the year in Sunday School. I know how you have worked over your lessons, how you have helped your teachers and how punctual you have been. To be sure, I know some of you haven't helped your teachers as much as you could have done, but I'll forget all that at Christmas time. Now tell me what you wish for most.

Children (*in audience who have previously rehearsed this scene*). A Christmas tree. A look at old Santa Claus. Some nice Christmas presents, etc.

Wishing Man. Stop, stop. I can't attend to so many wishes at once.

Little Girl (*rising*). Please, Mr. Wishing Man, couldn't you tell us what we'd better wish for?

Wishing Man. Have you ever had a great, big Christmas tree?

Children. Oh, yes, lots of times.

Wishing Man. Have you ever seen my old friend, Mr. Santa Claus?

Children. Oh, yes.

Little Boy. We see him every year at Christmas.

Wishing Man. How would like to go with me to Wishing Land.

Children. Oh, goody! (*Clapping hands.*) That would be fine. Can you take us there?

Wishing Man. Of course I can. And that's just what we'll do. We'll all of us go to the Wishing Land. First, I'll call little Dumpling. Dumpling, little Dumpling, where are you?

Big Dumpling *comes in from behind the curtains.*

Big D. Here I am, Mr. Wishing Man. I was playing with my little horse and wagon. (*He plays with tiny horse and wagon.*)

Wishing Man. And how do you like being a great, big Dumpling?

Big D. Well, not very well. I'm always bumping my head on the doors and things. And all my toys are so very little I'm always breaking them.

Wishing Man. Where is your sister? Where is little Tootsy?

Big Tootsy *enters.*

Big T. Here, Mr. Wishing Man. I'm here. Me and my little dolly.

Wishing Man. Well, little Tootsy, how do you like being a great, big Tootsy?

Big T. I don't like it very well. My clothes don't seem to fit, and I know I look awfully funny. (*To audience.*) Don't I? Everybody laughs at me and it always makes me cry. (*Cries.*)

Wishing Man. And where is little Snookie Ookums?

Big Snookums *enters.*

Big S. Here I am, Mr. Wishing Man. Here's 'ittie Snookie Ookums.

Wishing Man. You look like a 'ittie baby elephant, Snookie Ookums. Well, are you children satisfied with your wish?

The Three. Not very much. We wish we were little again.

Big S. (*crying*). I tried to ride my little horsie and I bweaked him all to pieces.

Big D. And I can't get enough to eat. My little knife and fork and spoon are too little, and when I eat I swallow dishes and all. (*Cries.*)

Big T. And all my clothes are too little for me, and I look so funny that everybody laughs at me. And I don't like it at all. (*Cries.*)

Wishing Man. I'm just going to start on a journey to the Wishing Land. The toys there are awfully big. They'd be just the right size for you. Would you like to go with me?

Big S. Is it very far?

Big D. Could we get back by bedtime?

Big T. Wouldn't it be awfully cold flying through the air?

Wishing Man. Oh, no. We'd fly so fast you'd only have time to shiver once and then we'd be right there.

The Three. Oh, yes; let's go.

Wishing Man. All right. Now all of you part your hair right in the middle, so you won't be heavier on one side than on the other. (*They do so.*) That's good. Now give me your hands and hold on tight and we're off to the Wishing Land. Follow me, full of glee.

(*All sing the first verse and chorus of "Follow Me, Full of Glee," accompanied by the children in the audience. At the end all dance off the stage at R.*)

Act III.

Scene: *The Wishing Land. Green or dark colored curtains at rear and at sides. Use all the large palms and potted trees available. A trumpet vine is attached to curtains at the rear. This is made of branches pinned on curtain to simulate a vine. Several tin trumpets are tied to the branches and many trumpets of various sizes made of paper. These stick out of the vines like*

blossoms.

At rear right is a large tree with buds made of tissue paper and toy drums showing in the buds. See diagram. The leaves forming these buds should be pointed oval in shape and vary in size as they represent buds or open flowers. The drums hang down from the branches and the petals, when open, hang open and partly cover them. Another tree stands at rear L. This is hung with candy or bits of colored paper simulating candy. Candy canes are on this tree and Jim Dandy *is sleeping at bottom of tree.*

At R. about half-way back are branches arranged to look as if growing, and about three feet high, hung with balls of various sizes and colors.

At L. about half-way back are three little girls dressed as French dolls. They stand in a row facing the audience. At either end of the row is a frame to support the cheesecloth curtain that hides them from the audience. They must stand stiffly with arms held out straight in front of them.

At L. front are several rows of flower pots or boxes containing growing plants with dolls fastened among the leaves. These are branches about eighteen inches high, with green paper buds partly enveloping the dolls.

At R. front is a large square box (a pasteboard cracker box or breakfast food box covered with red tissue paper will answer) in which is Ka-zin-ski *concealed by the lid.*

At R. half-way back just in front of the ball-trees stand three little boys dressed as toy soldiers. They stand erect and do not move.

Curtain rises to mysterious music played by piano. This continues some little time until the audience "takes in" the scene.

After a pause, enter the Wishing Man, *followed by the three* Big Children.

Wishing Man. Well, here we are in the Wishing Land. My kingdom and not a soul to welcome me!

Big D. Oh, what a beautiful, beautiful, beautiful place.

Big S. See 'ittie bitsy teeny weeny trumpets gwowing in twees.

Big T. And the dolls. The lovely, lovely dolls.

Wishing Man (*clapping his hands*). What, ho! Is there none to welcome me?

Enter Teddy Bear *from L.*

Teddy Bear (*comes to* Wishing Man *and bows low*).

Big D. Oh, see the Teddy Bear.

Big T. And he's the biggest one I ever saw.

Big S. Nice pussy, nice, nice pussy! (*Strokes* Teddy Bear.)

Teddy Bear (*growls*).

Big S. (*much frightened*). Oh, naughty, naughty, naughty!

Wishing Man. Hello, Teddy Bear. Where's your brother?

155

Teddy Bear (*shakes head as if he does not know*).

Wishing Man. Go out and find him for me. Have you been a very, very good Teddy Bear while I was away?

Teddy Bear (*nods his head*).

Wishing Man. That's good. Now go out and find Jimmy Bear.

Teddy Bear (*nods head and ambles out at R.*).

Wishing Man (*looking around*). Everything is growing fine. I think the bicycle trees need a little more water. Well, children, what do you think of the Wishing Land?

Big D. It's awfully pretty.

Big T. It's perfectly gorgeous.

Big S. Wunnerful, simply wunnerful.

Wishing Man. Here's where I grow my toys. See, there is the trumpet vine, and the candy tree and the dolly flowers. Whenever a little child makes a wish for anything like that, all I have to do is to come in here and pick a toy. See?

Big D. Oh, lookee at the tin soldiers. They're awful big. Can I have one, Mr. Wishing Man?

Wishing Man. I don't think they're quite ripe yet.

Big S. Me want a twumpet. Want a nice, big twumpet to blow.

Wishing Man (*picks a trumpet*). There you are, my little man.

Big T. I want one, too. A nice loud one.

Wishing Man (*picks one*). And there's one for you, Tootsy.

Big D. Believe I'll take a drum.

Wishing Man (*picks a drum*). There you are. Right off the tree.

Big D. Now we'll have a parade. (*They march around stage playing trumpets and drums.*)

Wishing Man. Here, here, wait a minute. You're making enough noise to wake the dead. Hold on, there. Quiet, quiet!

Big T. Oh, dear! Just as we were having such a lovely time.

Big S. Oh, whee! See the funny box. (*Goes to* Ka-zin-ski's *box.*) What is in it, Mr. Wishing Man?

Wishing Man. You'd better let it alone. That's Ka-zin-ski, and Ka-zin-ski doesn't like babies.

Big S. But I wish to see him.

Wishing Man. Is it a wish? Big S. Yes, sir; it's a wish.

Wishing Man. Then pull the string.

(Big S. *leans over the box, pulls a spring, the lid flies up and* Ka-zin-ski *pops out almost in the baby's face.* Big S. *screams and falls flat down on the stage.*)

Big S. Oh, whee! Take him away! I'm fwightened, I am. Vill he come after me?

Wishing Man. No, no. Get up, 'ittie Snookie Ookums, he won't hurt you.

Big D. Say, Mr. Wishing Man?

Wishing Man. What is it, my little boy?

Big D. Can we have anything we wish for here in the Wishing Land?

Wishing Man. Of course you can. That's what the Wishing Land is for.

Big D. Then I wish I was a little boy again. I'm too big to enjoy myself.

Big T. And I wish I was a little girl again. Everybody laughs at me, 'cause I'm so big.

Big S. And I wish I was a 'ittie, teeny, weeny baby again. Being so big fwightens me so.

Wishing Man. Oh, ho! So you all want to be little again?

The Three. Yes, sir, if you please.

Big T. Why, I'm so big that I can't get all of me into bed. I'll have to let my feet hang outside.

Big S. And if I get in my baby buggy, I'll bweak it all down.

Big D. And my mamma won't recognize me at all, 'cause I'm grown so big.

Wishing Man. That's all very well, but it will be quite a job to make you all little again. It will take three magic fern seeds, and I don't think I have any ripe yet.

(*Music, a march.* Teddy Bear *dances in in time to the music. He goes up to the* Wishing Man, *pulls his head down and whispers something in his ear. Then hands him a little box.*)

Big D. Oh, what is it, Mr. Wishing Man? Is it the fern seed?

Wishing Man (*looks in the little pill box*). Yes, but it's only one fern seed. Only one of you can be made little again.

Big D. Give it to my sister, Tootsy. She's a girl.

Big T. No, give it to Dumpling. He's the oldest.

Wishing Man. I think I'll give it to 'ittie Snookie Ookums. Here, Snookums, take that little seed and go down by the pump and get a drink of water. Put the seed in the water and swallow it and you'll be the original 'ittie Snookums again.

Big S. Oh, goody, goody, goody! (*Takes box and skips out at R.*)

(*Music again, a march.* Jimmy Bear *dances in, whispers to the* Wishing Man *and gives him a pill box.*)

Wishing Man. Here's another fern seed. Ladies first, Dumpling. I'll give it to Tootsy.

Big T. Oh, you dear, good Wishing Man. I'll give you a nice hug and kiss for that. (*Does so, takes box, skips out at R.*)

(*Music again. Enter* Baby Jumbo, *dancing in time to the music.* Wishing Man *bends down and whispers to the elephant.* Jumbo *raises one foot, a front one, and gives him a pill box.*)

Wishing Man. And here's the third magical fern seed. Here you are, Master Dumpling. Hurry along and grow little again.

Big D. Oh, thank you, sir. (*Takes box and skips out at R.*)

Jumbo *and the* Two Bears *dance out at L. in time to the music.*

Wishing Man (*goes to the doll bushes*). The dolly plants don't seem to be doing very well. (*Picks a doll.*) Here's a ripe one. I'm going to give that to (*insert some little girl's name*) for a Christmas present. And here's another for ——. I wonder how my big French dolls are doing. They're dreadfully hard to raise. They require so much attention. I have to keep them under cover to protect them from the sun. The wax melts so easily and the pretty red cheeks are apt to run down over their pretty French dresses. (*Removes cover.*) How nice they look. There's Annette, Olivette and Babette. Three as pretty little French ladies as ever came out of Paris. I think they're just about ready to pick. They're such pretty dollies that I think I'll give them to little boys instead of little girls. I'll give Annette to (*insert little boy's name*) and I'll give Olivette to ——, and little Babette I'll give to ——. My, my, I was forgetting all about the children and the mysterious fern seed. I wonder if it has changed them back into real little children again. (*Looks out at R.*) Yes, here they come.

Enter from R. Dumpling, Tootsy *and* Snookums.

Dumpling. Oh, thank you, Mr. Wishing Man. I feel ever so much better now.

Tootsy. Yes, indeed. My clothes are a perfect fit and nobody will laugh at me now.

Snookums. I feel perfectly fan-tas-a-ma-gor-ious.

Tootsy. Oh, see the pretty French dollies. I wish they would talk to me.

Wishing Man. If that's your wish, they can.

Tootsy (*presses* Annette). Can you talk?

Annette (*imitates talking doll*). Pa-pa, pa-pa, pa-pa!

Tootsy (*presses* Olivette). And what can you say?

Olivette. Ma-ma, ma-ma, ma-ma!

Snookums (*presses* Babette). Go on and talk to me.

Babette. Mer-ry Christ-mas! Mer-ry Christ-mas!

Tootsy. I wish you could wind them up so they could walk around and play with us.

Wishing Man. Is that your wish?

Tootsy. Oh, yes. Do you think you can do it?

Wishing Man. I can try. (*Takes large clock key and winds each doll. The sound of winding should be imitated by a rattle behind the scenes.*)

Annette. Pa-pa, pa-pa, pa-pa! (*Walks forward without bending knees.*)

Dumpling. Here, stop her. She'll fall down. (*Grabs her.*) Here, turn around. Walk this way. (*Walks with her.*)

Olivette. Ma-ma, ma-ma, ma-ma; (*Starts to walk.*)

Tootsy (*catches her*). Oh, I think you are a darling. (*Walks with her.*)

Babette. Mer-ry Christ-mas! Mer-ry Christmas. (*Starts to walk.*)

Wishing Man. Here, wait for me. (*Takes her arm and they walk together.*)

Dumpling. Wind up the soldiers. Then each dolly can have a partner.

Wishing Man. Just a minute. (*Winds up the soldiers.*)

(*The dolls continue walking around with jerky steps.*)

Private Black (*as* Babette *passes him*). Allow me. (*Offers her his arm.*)

Private Jack (*as* Annette *passes him*). Allow me. (*They promenade.*)

Private Mack (*as* Olivette *passes him*). Allow me. (*They promenade.*)

Tootsy (*very much excited, runs to* Wishing Man.) Oh, I wish they were all alive.

Wishing Man. You do? Is that your wish? (*She nods.*) Then I'll make them all alive.

Hickety, kickety, bees in a hive,
Witchery, twichery, you're alive.

(*The dolls and soldiers twirl around and chatter merrily in pantomime. Their actions from now on are as natural as possible.*)

Snookums (*suddenly sees the candy tree*). Oh, lookee! Candy!

Wishing Man. That's alive, too. (Jim Dandy *marches down.*) Mr. Snookie Ookums, let me introduce you to Mr. Jim Dandy, a stick of candy.

Snookums. Would he mind if I'd take a bite out of his leg?

Jim Dandy. You bet he would. I'm alive now.

Wishing Man (*looks off at L.*). And here comes Teddy Bear and Jimmy Bear. They're alive, too. And look at the Baby Elephant.*Enter* Teddy Bear, Jimmy Bear and Baby Jumbo. *The piano plays a march. All march around the stage, first the* Wishing Man, *then* Black *and* Babette, Jack *and* Annette, Mack *and* Olivette, Jim Dandy *and* Tootsie, Teddy Bear *and* Dumpling, *then* Baby Jumbo *with* Snookums *riding on his back, then* Jimmy Bear *capering in the rear. March around several times. A simple folk dance may be introduced at this point. All sing two verses of "Follow Me, Full of Glee."*

Curtain.

REMARKS ON THE PRODUCTION.

The room was all in shimmering white with a background of small pine trees in large wooden pots. The floor was covered with white muslin and scattered with leaves, pine needles and cones.

In one corner was a giant snow pile, made of a frame covered with cotton. This was presided over by the Snow Queen and her Maids and white-wrapped bundles were on sale for five cents.

Jack Frost and his boys presided over a large tree in another corner. Small toys wrapped in white tissue paper were attached to this tree and sold for five cents. Or Santa Claus may preside at the sale.

Snowballs of white popcorn and snowballs filled with candy were on sale at another booth, presided over by red and white Striped Candy Girls. Candy canes were also sold here.

In the fourth corner a snow scene in the woods was depicted. A local acrobat, dressed as a Snow-man, did stunts, assisted by several boys dressed as clowns. They pelted the Snow-man with snowballs and then sold bags of white confetti. The Snow-man also ran a game where snowballs were thrown at a target. The target was a circle of black cambric, the snowballs were rubber balls covered with raw cotton and rolled in flour. Balls sold three for five cents.

A postoffice in charge of Mrs. Santa Claus is recommended, where each pays five cents postage due for packages and postcards.

If snowballing the target is too "mussy," a large holly wreath with a cluster of sleighbells in the center may be suspended from the ceiling with red and green streamers. Three balls of soft rubber are provided and the contestants try to throw the balls through the wreath and ring the bells.

Stuffed stockings on a clothesline may be offered for sale. This should be presided over by Moll Pitcher and her colonial wash-maids.

A rummage sale of toys added quite a large sum to the general fund. There was a 5-cent table, a 10-cent table and a 25-cent table.

THE SCENERY FOR THE PLAY

The rear of the stage should be hung with dark curtains. Arrange the trumpet vine and the trees in place before the play begins. Then hide them with screens, these screens serving as the "scenery" for Act I.

During the progress of Act II, in front of the front curtain, remove the screens and furniture of Act I and arrange the stage for Act III as described in the text.

For the thunder effect in Act I rattle a large sheet of sheet-iron and explode several large fire-crackers.

The arrangement of the stage in Acts I and III is fully described in the text.

PROPERTIES.

Table with long cover completely hiding the Wishing Man.

Lighted lamp on table. Chairs and sofa.

Window at rear. Two curtains can simulate a window.

Trumpet vine with tin and paper trumpets.

Drum tree with tissue paper buds and toy drums.

Candy tree.

Ball plants.

Frame to hide the French dolls.

Doll plants.

Pasteboard box with cover for Ka-zin-ski.

Three small pill boxes.

COSTUMES

The Wishing Man—Dressed as a clown, white suit with red horseshoes on it. Red ruffles around arms, ankles and neck. Long, pointed, white clown cap. Face and neck should be covered with white grease paint and when it is dry apply white powder. Then blacken the nose and lips with hot black grease paint. Make tiny high eyebrows of this black paint and paint round black circles on cheek bones.

Grandpa, Grandma, Father and Mother should be dressed in modern costume, but they must be made up and costumed to look the part.

Nurse Maid—Black dress, long. White apron, collar, cap and cuffs.

Dumpling, Tootsy and Snookums—Pretty dresses suitable for Christmas.

The Big Dumpling, Tootsy and Snookums—Dressed exactly like their little counterparts. Wigs, etc.

Ka-zin-ski—Tall boy dressed as a clown. False face. Bushy whiskers and wig. A regular jack-in-the-box make-up.

The Tin Soldiers—Long trousers of shiny blue cambric with red stripes at the sides. Shiny red jackets with yellow bands and buttons across front and on sleeves. Toy guns. The cheeks and lips should be very red to imitate toy soldiers.

The French Dolls—Fancy dresses and bonnets. Hair in curls. Faces painted to represent wax dollies, red cheeks, eyebrows black, eyelashes beaded with black hot grease paint.

Jim Dandy—Red and white striped stockings. From the knee to under the arms the suit is a cylindrical roll of white pasteboard striped with red. Sleeves and collar white striped with red. Pointed white cap striped with red.

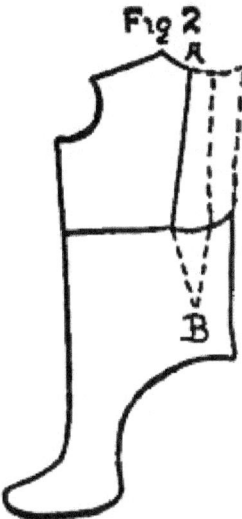

Fig 2

The Bears—Costumes of brown canton flannel, fuzzy side out. Get a pattern for a child's nightdress with feet. Allow it rather loose in front, so that a folded knit shawl can be securely fastened (with safety pins) to the shoulders in front, beneath it, thus making the round body of the bear. For the] back of the suit do not cut the waist part separate from the legs, as is usual in the pattern, but allow the waist to be as wide as the seat of the drawers.

Then lay a pleat from A to B on either side, tapering to form a loose fit below the waist. Sew thumbless mittens to the ends of the sleeves, padding them a little on the back and sewing on palms of a light tan, to represent paws.

Fit the seat of the drawers at the back loose enough to give freedom of motion, but no more.

For the heads, cut hoods like Fig. 3, taking a straight piece of cloth and fitting it with pleats around the face, etc. Make ears of two thicknesses of the cloth, stitched and turned like Fig. 4. Lay a box-pleat at A-B and sew them to the hood at C-D, so that they will stand out and forward. See Fig. 5. Sew this hood to the neck of the suit, so that all goes on together. Bear false faces.

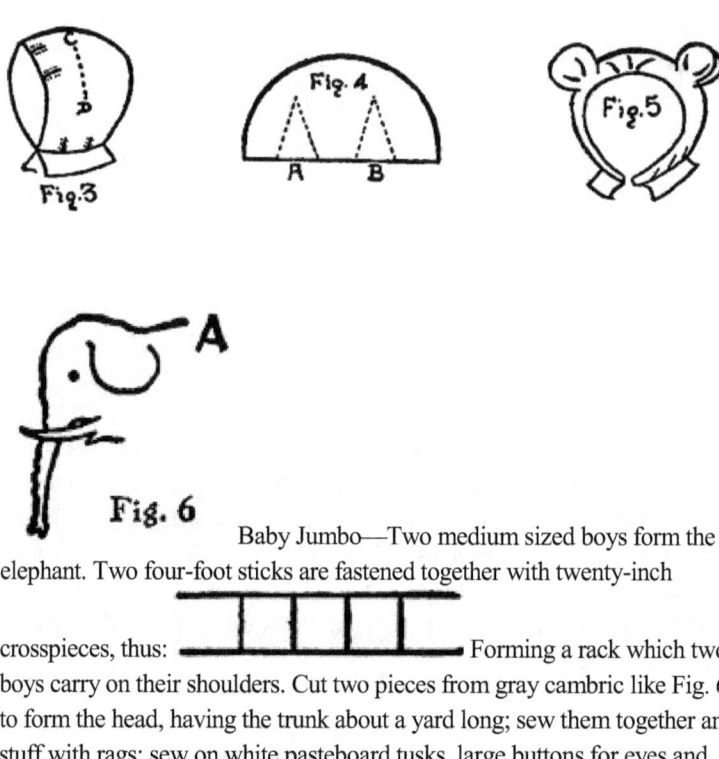

Fig. 3

Fig. 4

Fig. 5

Fig. 6

Baby Jumbo—Two medium sized boys form the elephant. Two four-foot sticks are fastened together with twenty-inch crosspieces, thus: Forming a rack which two boys carry on their shoulders. Cut two pieces from gray cambric like Fig. 6 to form the head, having the trunk about a yard long; sew them together and stuff with rags; sew on white pasteboard tusks, large buttons for eyes and big ears cut out of cambric and lined with one thickness of paper. Attach strings at A and tie to the first crosspiece of the rack. Pad the rack with an old comfort sewed fast with cord to hold it in place.

Set the rack on the boy's shoulders, then standing with heads bent forward, the foremost boy supporting the elephant's head with his head and slipping his right hand into the upper part of the trunk so as to swing it. Throw over them a large, dark-colored shawl, reaching to their knees, fasten it together in the back and pin on a tail made of cambric and stuffed. Legs covered with brown burlap.

A CHRISTMAS CAROL OR THE MISER'S YULETIDE DREAM

A CHRISTMAS CAROL OR THE MISER'S YULETIDE DREAM

ADAPTED FROM CHARLES DICKENS' IMMORTAL STORY.

CHARACTERS.

Ebenezer Scrooge
"Hard and sharp as flint, from which no steel had ever
struck out generous fire."

Bob Cratchit
"With the Christmas spirit in his heart."

Fred
"A whole-souled, merry-hearted young married man."

Two Mission Lassies

The Ghost of Jacob Marley
"Dead these seven years."

First Spirit (Little Girl)

Second Spirit

Third Spirit

A Chorus of Young Boys

First Wait

Mr. Fezziwig

Mrs. Fezziwig

Ebenezer

Dick

The Old Fiddler

Bella

Mrs. Cratchit

Belinda, *Aged Eighteen*

Martha, *Aged Seventeen*

Peter, *Aged Fourteen*

Bob, *Aged Eleven*

Betty, *Aged Nine*

Tiny Tim, *Aged Four*

Five Ladies, Five Gentlemen and a Little Boy for the Fezziwig Tableau

Stave I.

Scene: *The counting house of* Scrooge *and* Marley. *A dark, dreary office, indicated by brown curtains at sides, with entrances R. and L. and brown* *curtains at rear. Note: These rear curtains must be arranged to be parted, showing the tableau stage back of the real stage. The tableau stage is elevated a few feet above the real stage (this makes a better picture but is not absolutely necessary). High desk at R. facing the R. wall. Tall stool at this desk; ledger, quill pen, ink, candle on this desk. Small, old desk down L., facing audience. Desk chair back of this desk. Two common wooden chairs at R.C. and L.C. Ledger, quill pen, books, candle stuck in an old dark bottle, on desk down L.*

Full description of costumes, a detailed illustration of the stage setting, etc., will be found at the end of the play.

Before the curtain rises Waits *are heard singing off L. Curtain rises disclosing* Bob Cratchit *seated on stool, bent over ledger at desk R., working by the light of the candle.*

Waits (*outside, sing "Christmas Carol"*).

(Cratchit *turns and listens.*)

Enter Scrooge *from R. in a towering passion. Slams door R.* Cratchit *hurriedly returns to his work.* Scrooge *crosses to door L. and flings it open angrily.*

CHRISTMAS CAROL.

J. M. NEALE.
THOMAS HELMORE.

Maestoso.

1. Christ was born on Christ-mas day, Wreathe the hol - ly,
2. He is born to set us free; He is born our
3. Let the bright red ber - ries glow Ev - 'ry-where in

twine the bay, Light and life and joy is He, The
Lord to be; Car - ol, Chris-tians, joy - ful-ly; The
good - ly show, Light and life and joy is He, The

Babe, the Son, the Ho - ly One of Ma - ry.
God, the Lord, by all a - dored for - ev - er.
Babe, the Son, the Ho - ly One of Ma - ry.

Christian men, re-joice and sing; 'Tis the birth-day of our King.

Car - ol, Christians, joy - ful - ly; The God, the Lord, By

all a-dored For-ev - er. Night of sadness, Morn of glad-ness

Ev - er-more: Ev - er, Ev - er, Aft - er man - y

troub-les sore, Morn of glad-ness ev - er-more, and ev - er-more.

Mid-night scarce-ly passed and o - ver, Draw-ing to the

FINE.

ho - ly morn; Ver - y ear - ly, Ver - y ear - ly, Christ was born.

Piu lento.

Sing out with bliss, His name is this: Em - man - u - el!

a tempo.

D. S.

As 'twas fore-told, In days of old, By Ga - bri - el.

Scrooge (*flinging open door L. at this point*). Get away from my door. Begone, ye beggars! I've nothing for you.

First Wait (*sticking his head in door at L.*). Only a shillin', sir, for a merry Christmas, yer honor.

Scrooge. Get away from there or I'll call the police.

First Wait. Only a shillin', sir.

Scrooge. Not a penny. I have other places to put my money. Go on, now. You don't get a cent. Not a penny!

First Wait. All right, sir. Merry Christmas, just the same, sir. (*Exits L.*)

Scrooge (*comes down to his desk at L., muttering*). Howling idiots! Give 'em a shilling, hey? I'd like to give 'em six months in the work'us, that I would. Paupers! I'd show 'em what a merry Christmas is. (Cratchit *gets down from stool and starts to slink out L.*) Hey!

Cratchit (*pauses, turns to* Scrooge). Yes, sir.

Scrooge. Where you goin'?

Cratchit. I was just goin' to get a few coals, sir. Just to warm us up a bit, sir.

Scrooge. You let my coals alone. Get back to work. I'm not complaining about the cold, am I? And I'm an older man than you are. Back to work!

Cratchit (*sighs, pauses, then says meekly*). Yes, sir. (*Resumes work.*)

Scrooge. You want to let my coals alone if you expect to keep your job. I'm not a millionaire. Understand? (*Loudly.*) Understand?

Cratchit. Yes, sir, I understand. (*Shivers, wraps long white woolen muffler closer about throat and warms hands at candle.*)

Scrooge. Here it is three o'clock, the middle of the afternoon, and two candles burning. What more do you want? Want me to end up in the poorhouse?

Fred (*heard outside at L.*). Uncle! Uncle! Where are you? Merry Christmas, uncle.

Fred *enters from L. He is happy and bright and has a cheerful, loud laugh. He enters laughing and comes down C.*

Scrooge (*looking up from his work*). Oh, it's you, is it?

Fred. Of course it is, uncle. Merry Christmas! God save you!

Scrooge (*with disgust*). Merry Christmas! Bah! Humbug!

Fred. Christmas a humbug, uncle? You don't mean that, I'm sure.

Scrooge. I don't, hey? Merry Christmas! What cause have you got to be merry? You're poor enough.

Fred (*laughing good-naturedly*). Come, then, what right have you got to be dismal? You're rich enough. So, merry Christmas, uncle.

Scrooge. Out upon your merry Christmas! What's Christmas time to you but a time for paying bills without money; a time for finding yourself a year older, but not an hour richer? You keep Christmas in your own way and let me keep it in mine.

Fred. Keep it? But you don't keep it!

Scrooge. Let me leave it alone, then. Much good may it do you! Much good has it ever done you!

Fred. Christmas is a good time, uncle; a kind, forgiving, charitable, pleasant time; the only time I know of, in the long calendar of the year, when men and women seem by one consent to open their shut-up hearts freely, and to think of people below them in the social scale. And therefore, uncle, though it has never put a scrap of gold or silver in my pocket, I believe that it *has* done me good, and *will* do me good; and I say, God bless it, God bless Christmas!

Cratchit (*who had been listening eagerly, claps his hands*). Good!

Scrooge. Let me hear another sound from *you* and you'll keep your Christmas by losing your job. Get to work!

Cratchit. Yes, sir. (*Resumes his work on the ledger.*)

Scrooge (*to* Fred). You're quite a powerful speaker, sir. I wonder you don't go into Parliament.

Fred. Don't be angry, uncle. Come, dine with us tomorrow.

Scrooge. Dine with you? Me? I'll see you hanged first. Dine with you? I'll see you in—

Cratchit (*sneezes violently*).

Scrooge. What's the matter with *you*? (*Turns to* Fred.) I'm a busy man. Good afternoon.

Fred. Come, uncle; say "Yes."

Scrooge. No.

Fred. But why? Why?

Scrooge (*savagely*). Why did you get married?

Fred. Because I fell in love.

Scrooge. Bah! (*Resumes his work.*) Good afternoon.

Fred. I want nothing from you. I ask nothing from you. But why can't we be friends?

Scrooge. Good afternoon.

Fred. Uncle I won't part in anger. My dear mother was your only sister—your only relation. For her sake let us be friends.

Scrooge (*savagely*). Good afternoon.

Fred. I'll still keep the Christmas spirit, uncle. A merry Christmas to you.

Scrooge (*busy at ledger*). Bah!

Fred. And a happy New Year.

Scrooge. Good afternoon!

Fred (*goes to* Cratchit). And a merry Christmas to you, Bob Cratchit.

Cratchit (*getting down from stool, shaking hands with* Fred *warmly*). Merry Christmas, sir. God bless it!

Fred. Ay, God bless it! And a happy New Year.

Cratchit. And a happy New Year, too! God bless that, too!

Fred. Ay, Bob, God bless that, too. (*Exit L.*)

Scrooge. Cratchit, get to work!

Cratchit. Yes, sir. (*Resumes work.*)

Scrooge (*looks at him*). Humph! Fifteen shillings a week and a wife and six children, and he talks about a merry Christmas. Humph! (*Works on ledger.*)

Enter from L. Two Mission Lassies. *They come down C.*

First Lass. Scrooge and Marley's, I believe? Have I the pleasure of addressing Mr. Scrooge or Mr. Marley?

Scrooge. Mr. Marley has been dead these seven years. He died seven years ago this very night.

First Lass. We have no doubt his liberality is represented by his surviving partner. (*Shows subscription paper.*)

Scrooge. Liberality? Humph! (*Returns paper to her.*)

Second Lass. At this festive season of the year, Mr. Scrooge, we are trying to make some slight provision for the poor and destitute, who are suffering greatly. Hundreds of thousands are in want of common comforts, sir.

Scrooge. Are there no prisons?

Second Lass (*sighs*). Plenty of prisons, sir.

Scrooge. And the workhouses—are they still in operation?

First Lass. They are, sir; but they scarcely furnish Christmas cheer for mind and body. We are trying to raise a fund to buy the poor some meat and drink and means of warmth.

Second Lass. We chose this time because it is a time when want is keenly felt and abundance rejoices. What shall we put you down for?

Scrooge. Nothing.

First Lass. You wish to be anonymous?

Scrooge. I wish to be left alone. I don't make merry myself at Christmas, I don't believe in it. And I can't afford to make idle people merry. They should go to the poorhouse.

Second Lass. Many of them would rather die, sir, than do that.

Scrooge (*savagely*). If they would rather die, they'd better do it and decrease the population. And besides, I am a very busy man.

First Lass. But, sir—

Scrooge. Good afternoon.

First Lass. I'm sorry, sir. Sorry—

Scrooge. Sorry for them?

First Lass. No, sir, I'm sorry for you, sir. Good afternoon. (*Exits L. followed by* Second Lass.)

Scrooge. Sorry for me, hey? (*Pause. He works. The clock strikes five.*) Sorry for me!

Cratchit (*closes his book, blows out candle*). Is there anything more, sir? (*Comes to C.*)

Scrooge. You'll want all day off tomorrow, I suppose?

Cratchit. If it's quite convenient, sir.

Scrooge. Well, it isn't—and it's not fair. If I'd dock you a half a crown for it you'd think I was ill using you, wouldn't you?

Cratchit (*nervously*). I don't know, sir.

Scrooge. And yet you expect me to pay a full day's wages for no work.

Cratchit. It only comes once a year, sir. Only once a year.

Scrooge. A poor excuse for picking a man's pocket every twenty-fifth of December! But I suppose you've got to have the whole day. But you be here all the earlier next morning.

Cratchit. Oh, yes, indeed, sir. (*Goes out R.*)

Scrooge. I'll stay here a bit and finish up the work.

Enter Cratchit *from R. with hat. He turns up his coat collar, wraps the long white woolen muffler around chin and pulls hat down over his face.*

Cratchit (*crosses to door L.*). I'm going, sir.

Scrooge. All right.

Cratchit (*shields face with arm as though he were afraid Scrooge might throw something at him*). Merry Christmas, sir! (*Runs out L.*)

Scrooge. Bah! Humbug! (*He works at ledger. Finally drops his head on his arms and sleeps. The light of his candle goes out. Note: Scrooge might blow it out unseen by audience.*)

The stage is now in darkness. A musical bell tolls off L. After a pause another bell tolls off R. The clinking of chains is heard. When the stage is completely darkened the Ghost of Marley *slips in and sits at R. He is entirely covered with black, face and all, as he slips in, so as to be quite invisible.*

Mysterious music. Sudden clap of thunder heard. An auto light from the wings at R. is thrown on the Ghost's *face. This light should be green. The thunder dies away. Clanking of chains heard.*

Ghost (*groans*).

Scrooge (*starts up, looks at Ghost, pauses*). How now! What do you want with me?

Ghost. Much.

Scrooge. Who are you?

Ghost. Ask me who I was.

Scrooge. Well, who were you, then?

Ghost. In life I was your partner, Jacob Marley. It is required of every man that the spirit within him should walk abroad among his fellow-men, and if that spirit goes not forth in life, it is condemned to do so after death.

Scrooge. You are fettered. Tell me why.

Ghost. I wear the chain I forged in life. I made it link by link, yard by yard, the heavy chain of avarice. Now I must make amends for the opportunities I neglected in life.

Scrooge. But you were always a good man of business, Jacob.

Ghost. Business? Mankind should have been my business. Kind actions, charity, mercy, benevolence, love—all should have been my business. I am here tonight to warn you, to warn you, Ebenezer Scrooge, that you have yet a chance of escaping my fate.

Scrooge. You were always a good friend to me.

Ghost. You will be haunted by Three Spirits.

Scrooge. If it's all the same to you, I think I'd rather not.

Ghost. Without their visits, you cannot hope to escape my fate. Expect the first when the bell tolls one.

Scrooge. Couldn't I take it all at once and have it over, Jacob?

Ghost. Remember my warning, heed the message and you may yet be saved. My time is over. (*Chains rattle.*) Farewell, farewell, farewell! (*Loud crash of thunder. Light is quenched and* Ghost *exits unseen by audience.*)

Pause. The bell tolls one. Enter Spirit of Christmas Past *from R. She comes down R. Strong white light on her from R.*

Scrooge (*trembling*). Are you the Spirit whose coming was foretold to me?

First Spirit. I am.

Scrooge. Who and what are you?

First Spirit. I am the Ghost of Christmas Past.

Scrooge. Long past?

First Spirit. No, your past.

Scrooge. Why have you come here to me?

First Spirit. For your own welfare. I must teach you the first lesson of consideration.

Scrooge. But I *am* considerate.

First Spirit. Are you a kind master to your clerk?

Scrooge. Well, I'm not unkind.

First Spirit. Do you remember your own first master? One Fezziwig by name?

Scrooge. Indeed, I do. Bless his dear, old heart. He was the kindest master that ever lived.

First Spirit. Then why haven't you followed his good example? Would any of your clerks say that you were the kindest master that ever lived?

Scrooge. Well, times have changed, that's it—it's all the fault of the times.

First Spirit. It's all the fault of a squeezing, wrenching, grasping, scraping, clutching, covetous old sinner! Hard and sharp as flint, from which no steel has ever struck out a generous fire. No wind that blows is more bitter than he, no falling snow is more intent upon its purpose, no pelting rain less open to entreaty. And his name is Ebenezer Scrooge.

Scrooge. All I ask is to edge my way along the crowded path of life. I want to be left alone. That's all—left alone.

First Spirit. I have come to save you, Ebenezer Scrooge. I have come to kindle into life the stone that once was your heart. First I will show you the kind heart and generosity of your old time master. Behold the warehouse of Fezziwig and Company.

(*Rear curtains are drawn apart, revealing a workshop, with desk down R. facing front. Barrel up L. Sign on rear wall reads, "Fezziwig and Company." Two young men,* Ebenezer *and* Dick,*discovered happily working at desk. Fezziwig stands up L. looking off L.* Waits *are heard singing off L. at rear.*)

Waits

Christ was born on Christmas Day,
Wreathe the holly, twine the bay,
Light and Life and Joy is He,
The Babe, the Son,
The Holy One
Of Mary.

Fezziwig (*flinging them a handful of coins*). That's right, my lads. Sing away. Merry Christmas to you.

Waits (*outside*). Thank ye, sir. Merry Christmas and Happy New Year! Thank ye, sir. (*They sing and the song dies away in the distance.*)

Scrooge (*down R. with* First Spirit). Why, it's old Fezziwig. Bless his dear, old heart. It's Fezziwig alive again.

Fezziwig (*comes merrily down C.*). Yo ho, my boys! No more work for tonight. Christmas Eve, Dick! (*Throws his arms over the shoulders of the two boys.*) Christmas Eve, Ebenezer! God bless Christmas.

Dick. Ay, ay, sir.

Ebenezer. Ay, ay; God bless Christmas.

First Spirit. Did you hear that, Scrooge? That is yourself—and you said God bless Christmas.

Scrooge. That's true. That was thirty years ago.

Fezziwig (*bustling about*). The missis and the girls are down stairs, so let's clear away before you can say Jack Robinson. (*They push desk back, and decorate rear stage with strings of Christmas greens*, Fezziwig *talking all the time.*) Yo ho! That's right, Dick. String the Christmas greens. Here you are, Ebenezer. We're going to have the merriest time[Pg 182] in all the kingdom. (*Dancing a step or two.*) I'll show ye how to enjoy life. That's it. Now we're all ready. (*Sings.*) "Wreathe the holly, twine the bay!" Let's have lots of room. Clear away, Dick. Here comes the fiddler now.

Enter Old Fiddler. *He sits on barrel at rear and starts to "tune up."*

Old Fiddler. Merry Christmas, sir.

Fezziwig. The same to you, granfer, and many of 'em.

Enter Mrs. Fezziwig *from L.*

Mrs. Fezziwig. Lawsy, lawsy, I thought we'd be late. (*Goes to the two boys and puts her arms over their shoulders.*) And how's my merry boys tonight?

Dick. Finer'n a fiddle.

Ebenezer. Merry Christmas, Mrs. Fezziwig.

Mrs. Fezziwig. The same to you, dear lads.

Fezziwig. Where's the girls, mother?

Mrs. Fezziwig. Here they come, Flora, Felicity and little Fanny May.

Enter the Three Fezziwig *girls with their escorts. Everybody bustles around shaking hands, wishing each other "Merry Christmas."*

Fezziwig. And here's the housemaid and her cousin the baker. (*They enter and are greeted by all.*) The cook and the milkman, and the lonesome little boy from over the way! And Ebenezer's young lady, Miss Bella. (*They enter and are merrily greeted.*) And now, mother, what do you say to a rollicking game of Puss in the Corner.

(*They play Puss in the Corner with much loud laughter, clapping hands, running about, etc. The* Fiddler *plays.*)

Mrs. Fezziwig. Oh, I never was so happy in all my life. This is the real spirit of Christmas.

Fezziwig (*hangs up a bit of mistletoe*). And here's the mistletoe.

(*They form a ring and play a ring game with much noise and confusion.*)

Ebenezer (*catching* Mrs. Fezziwig *under the mistletoe*). I've got ye! (*Kisses her.*)

Mrs. Fezziwig. God bless the boy!

Ebenezer. And God bless the merry Christmas!

Fezziwig. And now a dance, my hearties. Yo ho! For the old time Christmas dance.

(*They dance a few figures of Sir Roger de Coverly or the Virginia Reel. All are dancing wildly, swinging, etc., with plenty of loud laughter, clapping of hands, etc., as the rear curtains are drawn. Note: Use brilliant lights from R. and L. upon the rear stage.*)

First Spirit. What a small matter to make these silly folks so full of gratitude and happiness.

Scrooge (*astonished*). Small? It was the happiest time in my life.

First Spirit. And yet your master only spent a few pounds of your mortal money. Three or four, perhaps. And yet he kindled the true spirit of Christmas in all your hearts.

Scrooge. He could have made us miserable, but he made every day we worked for him seem like Christmas.

First Spirit (*gazes steadily at Scrooge, who becomes uneasy under the look*). What's the matter now?

Scrooge (*trying to appear unconcerned, but failing*). Oh, nothing!

First Spirit (*gazing at him*). Something, I think.

Scrooge. No, nothing; only this, I wish I could say a word or two to my clerk just now. That's all. Poor fellow. I'm afraid I've been a little hard on him. Poor Bob Cratchit!

First Spirit. My work is thriving, but my time grows short. Quick, I have another picture for you.

Soft music. The curtains part, showing the scene as before, but only Ebenezer *and* Bella *are discovered. Soft music plays all through this scene.*

Bella. It matters little to you, very little. Another idol has displaced me, that's all. If it can comfort you and cheer you in time to come, as I would have tried to do, I have no just cause to grieve.

Ebenezer (*irritated*). What idol has displaced you in my heart?

Bella. An idol of gold.

Ebenezer. Well, I must make money. You know that. Poverty is the hardest thing in the world.

Bella. I have seen your nobler instincts fall off one by one. Now nothing remains in your heart but the love of gold. Therefore, I am releasing you from your engagement. (*Offers ring.*)

Ebenezer. Have I ever sought release?

Bella. In words, no; but in everything else, yes. I am penniless. If you married me, you would probably regret it. So I release you with a heart full of love for the noble man you once were.

Ebenezer. But, Bella—

Bella. You will soon forget me. Your time and your mind will be full of business, seeking after gold. The idol of gold has driven love from your heart, but may you be happy and contented in the life you have chosen. (*Rear curtains are drawn.*)

First Spirit. And are you happy and content in the life you have chosen, Ebenezer Scrooge?

Scrooge. No, a thousand times—no. I threw away her love, the one pure thing in my life, for gold. And now I'm alone, alone. (*Sinks at desk and sobs.*)

First Spirit. I have shown shadows of times that are passed. Have you learned a lesson from the Spirit of Christmas Past?

Scrooge. I have, I have; a bitter, bitter lesson.

First Spirit. And will you see more?

Scrooge. No, no. Show me no more. Torture me no longer.

First Spirit. Remember the lesson you have learned. Remember the kindness of your old master. Remember the love of your old sweetheart. Your life is barren and bitter, but there is yet time for repentance. (*Bell tolls twice.*) The signal! My hour is past. On the stroke of six my brother, the Spirit of the

Christmas Present, will visit you. Remember! Repent! Believe! Farewell, farewell, farewell!

Front Curtain Slowly Falls.

Stave II.

Same scene as Stave I. Lights half up, but candles are not burning. Rear curtains closed. Scrooge *is discovered asleep at his desk.*
The Spirit *of* Christmas Present *sits at R., a red light shining on him. He carries a torch in which a red light burns. The bells toll six times.* Scrooge *suddenly awakens and gazes at* Second Spirit.

Second Spirit. Arise, arise, Ebenezer Scrooge, and learn to know me better.

Scrooge (*frightened*). I don't believe I ever met you before.

Second Spirit. Probably not. I am the Spirit of Christmas. The Ghost of Christmas Present.

Scrooge. The Ghost of Christmas Present?

Second Spirit. I am a brother of the little Spirit of Christmas Past who visited you before.

Scrooge. And are you going to show me all my past misdeeds?

Second Spirit. Not me. I am going to show you your present misdeeds. It is my mission to show you the love and comradeship of Christmas of today. I travel among the common people. My torch is their benediction. If there is a slight quarrel or any misunderstandings on Christmas Day, I simply throw on them the light of my torch. And then they say it is a shame to quarrel on Christmas Day—the Day of Peace and Love. And so it is! God bless it! God bless Christmas Day!

Scrooge. And what do you intend to show me?

Second Spirit. I intend to show you the House of Happiness.

Scrooge. Is it a wonderful palace of gold?

Second Spirit. It is a humble little kitchen. In fact, the kitchen of your poor clerk, Bob Cratchit. Bob, with his fifteen shillings a week—with his wife and six children—with his shabby clothes and his humble, shabby manners—Bob, with his little four-roomed house, and his struggle to keep the wolf from the door. The Ghost of the Christmas Present blesses his abode. Behold!

Bright, cheerful music. Scrooge *and* Second Spirit *cross to R. The rear curtains open, showing the interior of the Cratchit kitchen. Everything neat, but showing extreme poverty. Fireplace C. rear. Kettle boiling on crane. Table down L.C. with red cloth and lighted lamp. Cupboard up R. Old chairs around stage. Several pots of bright flowers in evidence. A bird in a cage is singing over the mantel.* Peter *discovered watching the potatoes boiling in the kettle at the fireplace. Enter* Mrs. Cratchit *and* Belinda *from L.*

Mrs. Cratchit. Hurry, Belinda; we must set the table right away. How's the taters, Peter?

Peter (*peeks in the kettle*). Boiling, mammy, boiling.

Mrs. Cratchit. Here, carry the lamp over there.

Belinda. Yes, ma'am. (*Puts lamp on cupboard.*)

Mrs. Cratchit. And now where's the white table cloth?

Belinda (*getting it from cupboard*). Here it is, mammy. (*They place castor, plates, knives, etc., on table during the following scene.*)

Mrs. Cratchit. Whatever has got your precious father, I wonder? He and Tiny Tim's been at the church these three hours.

Enter Bob *and* Betty *from R. They run down and kiss* Mrs. Cratchit.

Bob. Oh, mumsy, we saw the goose, we did. We[Pg 188] peeked in through the bakery window and we saw the goose, we did.

Betty. And we smelled him, too. And we went inside, we did. And the baker asked us what was wantin'. And Bob said he wanted to know which goose was the Cratchit goose.

Bob. And he pointed to the very biggest one, mumsy. Didn't he, Betty?

Betty. And it was all nice and browny on top. And he said it 'ud be ready in 'bout twenty minutes. Didn't he, Bob?

Bob. And it was the best looking goose I ever saw, it was. It just made me hungry to see him and to smell him baking.

Betty. And it had sage and onion stuffing, mumsy, didn't it, Bob?

Mrs. Cratchit. I'm sure there never was such a goose before, and I'm sure there never will be such a goose again. How's the 'taters, Peter?

Peter (*looks in kettle*). Boilin', mammy, boilin'.

Bob. Oh, Peter's got on pa's shirt collar, he has. Peter's got on pa's shirt collar.

Peter. If I didn't have to mind these 'taters, I'd show you!

Mrs. Cratchit. I can't think what's keeping your father, and your brother Tiny Tim. And Martha wasn't as late last Christmas Day by half an hour.

Enter Martha *from R.*

Martha. Here's Martha, mumsy.

Bob (*dragging her down to Mrs. Cratchit*). Here's Martha, mumsy.

Betty. Oh, Martha, there's such a goose! Isn't there, Bob?

Mrs. Cratchit (*hugging and kissing* Martha). Why, bless your heart alive, my dear, how late you are! (*Takes off her bonnet and shawl.*)

Martha. We'd a deal of work to finish up last night. I was on my feet all day. Oh, why won't people learn to do their Christmas shopping early. If they'd only stop to give a moment's thought to the poor clerks.

Mrs. Cratchit. There, there, my dear, sit ye down. Here's the big chair, Martha. (Bob *has been sitting in the big chair at R., but* Mrs. Cratchit *simply turns it forward, letting* Bob *slip to the floor, and seats* Martha *therein.*) Well, never mind, as long as you're home at last, Martha. Draw your chair up to the fire and have a warm. God bless you. How's the 'taters, Pete?

Peter (*looking in kettle*). Boilin', mammy, boilin'.

Martha (*sitting in front of the fire*). Oh, mumsy, ain't this Heavenly? Be it ever so humble there's no place like home.

Betty (*at door R.*). Father's coming, father's coming.

Bob. Hide yourself, Martha. Here, here. (*Pulls her to L.*)

Betty (*helping her*). Hurry up. Hide, hide! (*Exit* Martha *at L.*)

Bright music. Enter Cratchit *carrying* Tiny Tim *on his shoulder.* Tiny Tim *carries a little crutch.*

Cratchit (*down C.*). Why, where's our Martha?

Mrs. Cratchit (*down L.*). Not coming.

Cratchit. Not coming? Not coming—on Christmas Day?

Martha (*rushing in from L.*). No, father, it's only a joke. Here I am, father, here I am. (*Rushes into his arms.*)

Betty (*taking Tiny Tim*). Come on, Tiny Tim, out to the wash-house. We've got something to show you, we have. Ain't we, Bob?

Bob. You bet we have, Tiny Tim. Come and hear the Christmas pudding singing in the wash boiler. Come on! (*Exit* Bob, *followed by* Betty *and* Tiny Tim, *at L.*)

Mrs. Cratchit (*taking Cratchit's hat and muffler and hanging them up*). And how did Tiny Tim behave in the church, father?

Cratchit. As good as gold and better. Somehow he gets thoughtful, sitting by himself so much, and thinks the strangest things you ever heard. (*Sits at L. surrounded by all.*) He told me, coming home, that he hoped the people saw him in the church, because he was a cripple, and it might be pleasant to them to remember upon Christmas Day, who it was who made lame beggars walk and blind men see. (*Trembling voice.*) Little Tim is growing stronger and more hearty every day.

Enter Tiny Tim *from L.*

Tim. I heard the pudding singing a song in the wash boiler, I did.

Mrs. Cratchit. Everything is ready. Bob, you and Betty run across the street to the baker's and fetch the goose.

Bob. Come on, Betty. (*Runs out R. with* Betty.)

Mrs. Cratchit. I've got the gravy to heat, right away. Peter, mash the potatoes. Belinda, sweeten up the apple sauce! Martha, the hot plates! (*All bustle around, setting table.* Cratchit *with* Tim, *on his knee, sit before the fire.*)

Belinda. We haven't got enough chairs, mumsy.

Cratchit. This young shaver can sit on my knee.

Mrs. Cratchit. Peter, set up the chairs.

Enter Bob *and* Betty *from R. bearing a roast goose in a baking pan.*

Bob. Here it is, mumsy.

Betty. Here's the goose. (Mrs. Cratchit *puts it on plate on table.*)

Belinda. What a wonderful goose.

Martha. And how big it is! (*All take seats.*)

Bob. And don't it smell good!

Betty. Hurray for the Christmas goose.

Tim. Hurray! (Cratchit *makes signal, all bend heads for a silent grace.*)

Cratchit (*after pronounced pause*). And God bless Christmas Day.

Tim. God bless us all, every one. (Cratchit *and* Mrs. Cratchit *serve the meal. All eat.*)

Cratchit. I've got a situation in my eye for Master Peter.

Peter. A situation for me?

Cratchit. Yes, sir, for you. Full five-and-sixpence weekly.

All. Oh, Peter!

Bob. Peter will be a man of business, won't you, Peter?

Peter. What'll I do with all that money?

Cratchit. Invest it, invest it, my lad. It's a bewildering income.

Martha. Who do you think was in the shop yesterday? You'll never guess. A countess and a real lord.

All. Martha!

Martha. A real, live lord, as fine as silk and just about as tall as Peter here.

Peter (*pulls his collar up high and tosses his head*). As big as me?
(Waits *outside sing two verses of Christmas Carol, as before.*)

Cratchit (*goes to door*). Here's a sixpence for you, and God bless you all.

Waits (*outside*). Thankee, sir. Merry Christmas, sir.

Belinda. And now the pudding.

Betty. Oh, suppose it should break in turning it out.

Martha. Or suppose it isn't done enough.

Bob. Suppose somebody should have got over the wall of the backyard and stolen it while we were in here eating the goose.

Mrs. Cratchit. Nonsense. I'll get the Christmas pudding. (*Exits.*)

Bob (*very much excited*). Oh, I can smell it, I can. I smell the pudding.

Enter Mrs. Cratchit *bearing dish of pudding, decked with holly, and blazing.*

Cratchit. Oh, it's a wonder, mother, it's a wonder.

Betty. It looks like a little speckled cannon-ball.

Bob. But just wait till you taste it; that's all. (*It is served.*)

Cratchit (*rises*). I have a toast. Mr. Scrooge! I'll give you Mr. Scrooge, the founder of the feast.

Mrs. Cratchit (*indignantly*). The founder of the feast indeed! I wish I had him here. I'd give him a piece of my mind to feast upon, and I hope he'd have a good appetite for it.

Cratchit (*remonstrating gently*). My dear, the children! Christmas Day.

Mrs. Cratchit. He's an odious, stingy, hard, unfeeling man. You know he is, Robert. Nobody knows it better than you do.

Cratchit (*mildly*). My dear, Christmas Day!

Mrs. Cratchit. Then I'll drink his health, for your sake and the Day's, not for his. Long life to him! A Merry Christmas and a Happy New Year! He'll be very merry and happy, I've no doubt.

Cratchit. And now a Merry Christmas to us all, my dears. God bless us.

All (*rising*). A very Merry Christmas.

Tim. And God bless us every one!

(*The tableau curtains are slowly drawn.*)

Scrooge. Spirit, tell me if Tiny Tim will live.

Second Spirit. I see a vacant seat in the poor chimney-corner, and a little crutch without an owner. If these shadows remained unaltered by the future, the child will die.

Scrooge. No, no, kind Spirit! Say he will be spared.

Second Spirit. If he be like to die, he had better do it, and decrease the surplus population. Your very words, Scrooge. Decrease the surplus population. (Scrooge *hangs his head in shame.*) Man, if man you be in heart, forbear that wicked cant. Will you decide what men shall live, and what men shall die? It may be that in the sight of Heaven you are more worthless and less fit to live than millions like this poor man's child.

Scrooge. Forgive me, forgive me.

Second Spirit. You have seen the spirit of Christmas bless this poor dwelling. They were not a handsome family, they were not well dressed; their clothes were scanty and their shoes far from being water-proof—but they were happy, grateful, pleased with one another, and contented with the Christmas time. They are my children. Have you learned your lesson? (*Chimes ring.*) My hour is spent.

Scrooge. I have learned the lesson, Spirit of Christmas. I have seen happiness, in spite of poverty. A happiness that all my gold cannot buy. I have seen the Christmas spirit. Forgive me that I ever dared to utter a word against Christmas. Forgive me! Forgive me! (*The chimes continue ringing, the* Spirit *glides out.* Scrooge *kneels in prayer, muttering, "Forgive me! Forgive me!"*)

Curtain.

Stave III.

Same scene as before, the rear curtains drawn together. Scrooge *is discovered seated at his desk, his head buried in his hands. The* Third Spirit *stands at C. with green, ghastly light on him from R. This is the only light on the stage. The bells toll six.*

Scrooge (*awakens*). I am in the presence of the Ghost of Christmas Yet to Come.

Third Spirit (*inclines head*).

Scrooge. You are going to show me the shadows of things that are to happen in the future?

Third Spirit (*inclines head*).

Scrooge. I fear you more than any I have yet seen. But I know you are working for my welfare, so I will see your visions with a thankful heart. Will you not speak to me?

Third Spirit (*points downward with R. hand*).

Scrooge. No word for me. Well, have you anything to show me?

Third Spirit (*points to rear stage. The curtains part. Rear stage is draped in white sheets, with bare trees at R. and L. A grave with carved headstone is at C. Blue lights on this scene. Snow falls. Bells heard tolling in the distance.*)

Scrooge. A churchyard!

Third Spirit (*goes to rear stage, points to tombstone.*)

Scrooge. Before I draw nearer to that stone to which you point, answer me one question. Are these the shadows of the things that Will be, or are they the shadows of things that May be, only?

Third Spirit (*points to stone*).

Scrooge (*creeps tremblingly toward it, moving very slowly, bends over, reads the name, screams*). Ebenezer Scrooge! My tombstone, my grave! No, Spirit, no, no! (*Rushes to desk, sinks in chair.*) I am not the man I was. I am not past all hope. I will honor Christmas in my heart, and try to keep it all the year. Save me, save me!

(*The rear curtains are slowly closed*)

Scrooge (*rising*). I will keep Christmas in the past, the present and the future. The spirits of all three shall strive within me. Heaven be praised for this Christmas warning. (*Laughing.*) I don't know what to do. I'm as light as a feather, I'm as happy as an angel, I'm as merry as a schoolboy. A Merry Christmas to everybody. A happy New Year to all the world. Hip, hurrah!

(*Christmas chimes heard outside. Waits singing in the distance.*)

Waits (*singing louder, music, page 169*):

Christ was born on Christmas Day,
Wreathe the holly, twine the bay,
Light and Life and Joy is He,
The Babe, the Son,
The Holy One
Of Mary.

Scrooge (*rushes to the door*). Merry Christmas, Merry Christmas. God bless ye! (*Flings them a handful of coins.*)

First Wait. Thankee, sir.

Scrooge (*grabs him and brings him down C.*). What day is this, my merry lad?

Wait. Hey?

Scrooge. What day is this my lad?

Wait (*loudly*). Today! Why, Christmas Day!

Scrooge. Do you know the grocer's in the next street?

Wait. I should hope I did.

Scrooge. Do you know whether they've sold the prize turkey that was hanging up there? Not the little prize turkey, the big prize turkey?

Wait. What, the one as big as me?

Scrooge. Yes, my buck.

Wait. It's hanging there now.

Scrooge. Is it? Go and buy it.

Wait. Aw, go on!

Scrooge. No, no; I'm in earnest. Go and buy it and tell 'em to bring it here, that I may tell 'em where to take it. Come back with the man, and I'll give you a shilling. Come back with him in less than five minutes, and I'll give you half-a-crown.

Wait. Watch me. (*Rushes out.*)

Scrooge. What a fine little fellow. See him run. I'll send the turkey to Bob Cratchit's. He shan't know who sends it. It's twice the size of Tiny Tim. He should be here by now.

Enter Cratchit *from R.*

Cratchit. Morning, sir. (*Takes off cap and muffler, goes to desk, starts to work.*)

Scrooge (*at desk*). What do you mean by coming here at this time of day?

Cratchit. I'm very sorry, sir. Very, very sorry.

Scrooge. Sorry? (*Sarcastically.*) Yes, you are! Come here! Come here at once! Understand!

Cratchit (*comes to Scrooge's desk*). If you please, sir—

Scrooge. I'm not going to stand this sort of thing any longer. And therefore (*rises, dances toward* Cratchit, *digs him in ribs*), and therefore I am about to raise your salary.

Cratchit. Heavens! The master has gone plumb crazy.

Scrooge. I'm going to help you and your family. I'm going to be a Godfather to all of 'em. The two girls and Master Peter, Bob, Betty and to dear Tiny Tim. Home to your family, now. Home to them, Bob Cratchit—and merry Christmas to you and yours. God bless you.

Enter Fred *from R.*

Fred. Here I am again, uncle. Merry Christmas.

Scrooge (*rushes to him and shakes his hands heartily*). And the same to you, my lad, and many of 'em. I'm going to eat Christmas dinner with you this day. I'm going to honor Christmas in my heart, and keep it every day in the year. I will live in the past, the present and the future. The spirits of all three shall strive within me. (*Stands C., Fred on his R., Cratchit on his L. He takes their hands.*) Merry Christmas, boys, and God bless us!

Fred *and* Cratchit. The same to you, sir. God bless us.

(*Rear curtains are drawn back, showing the Cratchit family at the table. Tiny Tim stands on table.*)

Tim. God bless us everyone!

(*All unite in singing Christmas Carol to—*)

Slow Curtain.

THE SCENERY.

TABLEAUX ON REAR STAGE.

No. 1. A room. Barrel up L. for fiddler. Desk at R. Sign on wall "Fezziwig and Company." Garlands of green.

No. 2. Ebenezer and Bella. Same scene as No. 1.

No. 3. Cratchit's kitchen. Table at C. and home-made fireplace at rear C. are the only essentials, with a few stools or chairs. Fireplace made of a few boards covered with red paper marked like bricks with white chalk or paint.

No. 4. White sheets hang at back and sides. Two small evergreen trees nailed in position, white cotton hanging from them. Grave at C. covered with snow. Wooden headstone painted white and small footstone. The headstone may be in the form of a cross or a slab.

COSTUMES

Scrooge—Should be played by a thin man of middle age, if possible. Gray hair. Shabby dark suit. Face lined. No jewelry or colors. If desired to costume the play in the middle Victorian period, Scrooge should wear very tight dark trousers, brown low cut vest, shabby black full-dress coat, soft white shirt, black stock tie, high collar made by taking an ordinary turn-over collar and turning it up.

Bob Cratchit—Very shabby dark suit. Long white woolen muffler. Old cap. Suit should be the same style as that worn by Scrooge, but much shabbier. Clothing neatly patched. He wears a sprig of mistletoe or holly in Staves 1 and 2.

Fred—Bright, cheerful young man of 22. Overcoat and top hat. Ruffled shirt, stock tie and collar as for Scrooge.

Mission Lassies—Dark skirts, capes, blue poke bonnets with red ribbon across front.

The Ghost of Jacob Marley—Long black robe. Black hood. Chains around waist, with toy money banks on chains. Take a skeleton false face and with gray and black and white grease paint make up your own face like a false face. Or if desired, wear the false face. Speak in low monotone.

First Spirit—A little girl of 10. Long light hair. White Grecian draperies trimmed with tinsel. Crown of tinsel.

Second Spirit—Man dressed in a red robe, trimmed with sprigs of green pine. White cotton border to represent snow. Cap of white cotton.

Third Spirit—Use same costume and make-up as Marley's Ghost.

Waits—White smocks, ragged trousers. Felt hats twined with red and green ribbon. Carry branches of holly.

Mr. Fezziwig—Low shoes with pasteboard buckles covered with tinfoil. Short black trousers. White stockings. Fancy colonial coat and hat. White colonial wig. A short, stout man of middle age. Always laughing, moving around, etc.

Mrs. Fezziwig—Middle-aged lady in gay colonial tuck-up dress. White colonial wig.

Ebenezer and Dick—Two young men in colonial costume. No wigs.

The Fiddler—White wig and whiskers. Long white smock. Hat trimmed with ribbons.

Bella—Neat colonial costume of pink and white. Hair in curls.

The Cratchit Family—Old-fashioned costumes, faded and worn, but bright with cheap lace and gay ribbons. Peter wears a large white collar.

HER CHRISTMAS HAT

WARREN WILLIAMS · KITTY, HIS WIFE · MISS MINERVA MOCKRIDGE
MAGINNIS GOOGIN · EDDIE · MRS HONORIA GOOGIN
MRS LAURA LACEY · HOGAN · HARD TIMES ANNIE

207

HER CHRISTMAS HAT

A FARCE IN ONE ACT.

HER CHRISTMAS HAT

A FARCE IN ONE ACT

CHARACTERS

Warren Williams A Young Architect

Kitty   His Wife

Miss Minerva Mockridge   From Kankakee

Maginnis Googin The Janitor of the Apartment

Mrs. Honoria Googin   His Wife

Eddie   The Elevator Boy

Mrs. Laura Lacey   Kitty's Chum

Hogan   A Policeman

Hard Times Annie   A Beggar

Time of Playing—*About Forty-five Minutes.*

Scene: *Living room in an apartment house. Furnishings as desired. Several Christmas wreaths adorn the room. Kitty is discovered comfortably seated down L. reading a fashion magazine. The door bell at R. rings.*

Kitty. Come in.

Enter Eddie, the colored elevator boy. He carries several Christmas packages.

Eddie. Yas'm, I'm in.

Kitty. Eddie!

Eddie. Yas'm, it's me. I 'clare I's loaded up like a reg'lar old Santa Claus. (*Laughs loudly.*) Yas'm, I sure am.

Kitty. Anything for us, Eddie?

Eddie. Two packages for you and one for Mr. Williams. Santa Claus is sure liberal to you-all.

Kitty (*taking the three packages*). Thank you, Eddie.

Eddie (*briskly*). I don't usually bring up de mail, Mis' Williams, but this is Christmas Day and mos' everybody is anxious to git all dat's comin' to 'em. I knows I is.

Kitty. Have you had a merry Christmas, Eddie?

Eddie. No'm, not yet. All I got is a yaller and green striped necktie from (*insert local name*). He's been wearin' it for more'n a year.

Kitty (*has opened smaller package*). Oh, it's from Rannie Stewart. (*Takes off tissue paper, disclosing a small bit of white embroidery tied with a huge pink bow.*) Mercy! Another pin-cushion cover. That makes six I have already. Cost about twenty cents, and I sent her a perfectly lovely doily embroidered with scarlet forget-me-nots. I'll never send Rannie Stewart another present as long as I live. (*Throws box and wrappings into waste basket.*) Pink! And she knows my rooms are in blue and yellow. Eddie!

Eddie. Yas'm.

Kitty. Here's a little Christmas present for you. (*Hands it to him.*)

Eddie (*reads card on it*). "Merry Christmas to my Darling Kittens." Is dat for me?

Kitty. Oh, no; not the card, just the embroidery.

Eddie (*holding it up*). Lawdy, Mis' Williams, what is dis yere? A dust cap?

Kitty. It's a cover for a pin-cushion. Isn't it a dear?

Eddie. I hopes you'll excuse me, but honest I hain't got no more use for dat thing dan a pussy cat has for a hot water bottle.

Kitty (*opening larger package*). Throw it in the waste basket, Eddie. This is from Warren. I know the handwriting. It looks like a hat. (*Opens box and removes wrappings, disclosing a hideous red and orange hat.*) Heavens, what a nightmare! Red and orange and a style four years old. It must have come from the five and ten cent store. Look at the plume! Oh!

Eddie (*admiring it*). Um-um, dat shore am a fine present. Your husband certainly am a man ob taste, he shore am.

Kitty (*sarcastically*). Yes, he has wonderful taste, hasn't he? A little bizarre. No, it's more than bizarre; it's baroque.

Eddie. It looks like a hat to me.

Kitty. I know what I'll do. (*Wraps it up and puts it back in box.*)

Eddie. Dat certainly was a nice present, Mis' Williams. Must have cost a heap of money.

Kitty. It probably did. But it isn't my style. And Madame Brunot never exchanges hats. What a shame! I suppose he paid an enormous price for it and I could have satisfied myself with one for half the money. If only men would allow their wives to select their own Christmas presents.

Enter Laura Lacey *from R.*

Laura. Hello, Kittens. I saw your door open and came right in.

Kitty (*kisses her*). That's right, Lolly. I was just going over to your apartment. I have a little present for you.

Laura. A present? You dear! (*Kisses her again.*)

Kitty. Yes. Here! (*Gives her the box containing the hat.*) I hope you'll like it.

Laura. A hat? Oh, you darling! (*Kisses her again.*)

Warren (*outside L.*). Kitty!

Kitty (*goes to door at L.*). Yes, Warren?

Warren. I can't find my collar button.

Kitty. Did you look on the dresser?

Warren. Of course I did. I've looked every place except in the refrigerator.

Kitty. I'll be back in a minute, Laura. Excuse me. (*Hurries out L.*)

Laura (*opens the box hastily and takes out the hat*). Red and orange! Horrors! And I gave her a cut glass cold-cream jar that I got at the auction. I wouldn't wear this to a dog fight. Eddie!

Eddie. Yas'm.

Laura. You've been a good boy to us all year. I'm going to give you a lovely Christmas present.

Eddie. Is you?

Laura. I'm going to give you this duck of a hat. (*Holds it up.*)

Eddie (*delighted*). Dat red and yaller hat?

Laura. Yes. Hurry and put it in the box. I don't want Kitty Williams to know I gave her Christmas present away. (*They put it in box.*)

Eddie. Um-um! Dat shore am some Christmas present. Won't ma lady-love be delighted with all dat gorgeousness? I certainly am much obliged to you, Mis' Lacey; I shore am.

Laura. When Kitty comes back tell her I was called to the 'phone. (*Goes to door R.*) I'll never give Kitty Williams another present as long as I live. (*Exits R.*)

Enter Warren Williams *from L.*

Warren. Hello, Eddie. Are you acting as Santa Claus?

Eddie (*who has put the hat on floor at rear*). Yas, sah; yas, sah. I's old Santa Claus to most everybody 'cept maself. Looks like old Christmas done passed me by.

Warren (*sees package on table*). Hello, here's a present for me.

Eddie. Yas, sah. I brung it up.

Warren (*opens it*). Cigars! From my wife. (*Looks at box dubiously.*) She must have got them at a bargain sale. (*Reads cover.*) Santas Odoriferous. (*Passes box to Eddie.*) Have a cigar, Eddie.

Eddie. Yas, sah. Thank you, boss.

Warren (*lighting one*). Now, that certainly is a sensible present. So many women don't know how to select a cigar, but Kitty—

212

Eddie (*smoking*). Yas, sah. Your wife certainly am a lady ob discernibility. She shore am.

Warren. So many women give their husbands such foolish presents.

Eddie. De lady in Apartment B done give her husband a pearl La Valliere for Christmas.

Warren (*takes cigar from mouth, looks at it a moment, replaces it and smokes furiously*). You like a good cigar, don't you, Eddie?

Eddie (*removes his cigar, looks at it, replaces it*). Yas, sah. I likes a *good* cigar.

Warren. I tell you these are something like cigars, aren't they?Eddie. Yas, sah. Dey's sumpin like 'em, boss, but not quite.

Warren (*chokes and then throws cigar in cuspidor*). I don't believe I care to smoke just now.

Eddie (*does the same*). Neither does I, boss; neither does I.

Warren. You wouldn't like a nice box of cigars for a Christmas present, would you, Eddie?

Eddie (*slowly*). No, sah, I don' 'spects I would. Ma lady-love don't like to hab me smoke no cigars, kase she says it contaminates ma presence. Well, I's got to go and deliber de res' ob my Christmas packages. Merry Christmas, boss. (*Exit R., carrying the hat in the box.*)

Enter Kitty *from L.*

Kitty. Warren, I've laid out the costumes in your room. They're too lovely for anything.

Warren. Well, did you get it?

Kitty. Get it?

Warren. Your Christmas present.

Kitty. Oh, yes, I got it. (*Looks around.*) Why, where is Lolly?

Warren. She probably got tired of waiting and went back to her apartment. How did you like the hat?

Kitty. It was a dream. You're such a good boy and you have the most wonderful taste in the world.

Warren. Your cigars were just what I wanted.

Kitty. Why aren't you smoking one?

Warren. I did. Just one.

Kitty. Just one?

Warren (*hastily*). I mean—I only smoke one cigar in the afternoon, you know. But where is your hat?

Kitty. I'm going to have it fixed over a little, Warren. Just enough to suit my own individuality, you know.

Warren. Jack Dawson gave his wife a cook stove.

Kitty. Speaking of impossible presents, I just got the most horrible pin-cushion cover from Rannie Stewart. I threw it in the waste basket.

Warren. That's what comes of promiscuous giving. I told you how it would be. First I decided not to buy anything at all, but I couldn't resist that hat. Your tickets to the masquerade dinner and ball are the rest of the present.

Kitty. But I told Lolly we'd take tickets from her.

Warren. I know. I haven't bought the tickets yet. I meant the money for them was the rest of your present. That and the hat. All my presents are beautiful practical things that every one wants.

Kitty. Yes, that's so. You have wonderful taste.

Warren. I didn't even give Eddie anything.

Kitty. It doesn't matter. Oh, Warren. (*Sits on arm of his chair.*) I'm so glad we're going to have tonight all to ourselves. Aunt Minerva would have spoiled everything.

Warren. Is she so very awful?

Kitty. Not awful; just good. Real downright good. And so intellectual. I'm sure she'd never approve of a Christmas masquerade.

(*Ring at the bell at R.*)

Kitty. See who it is.

Warren *admits* Maginnis Googin *from R.*

Googin. Merry Christmas, sor.

Warren. The same to you, Googin.

Googin. I jest drapped in to see if you naded any more heat or anything like that. My, my, but I've been working hard the day. Sure, to be the janitor of an apartment house is no cinch at all, at all. And paple are not as liberal as they used to be, aven at Christmas time.

Warren. Have a cigar.

Googin. Thank ye, sor. (*Smokes one.*)

Kitty. Warren, you'd better try on your costume. I might have to change something, you know.

Warren. But I—

Kitty. Please. We haven't got much time. It's after four.

Warren (*crosses to left*). All right. (*Exits L.*)

Kitty. Now, Mr. Googin, I want you to go down stairs and tell your wife to come up. I have a nice little present for her.

Googin (*brightening*). Have ye, now? A prisint for Honoria? Sure, it's a kind and thoughtful lady ye are.

Kitty. She's at home, isn't she?

Googin. She is that.

Kitty. Ask her to come up here and wish us a merry Christmas.

Warren *appears at L.*

Warren. Kitty, how does that ruffle thing work? I can't get it around my head at all. I don't know the combination.

Kitty. Oh, I must have sewed it together. Can't you get it over your head?

Warren. Not without choking myself.

Kitty. Wait a minute. I'll rip it for you. (*Exits L.*)

Warren (*gets box of cigars and hands it to Googin*). Here's a little Christmas present, Googin. They're awfully good. I smoked two of them.

Googin (*lights one*). Thank ye, sor.

Warren. Don't let my wife see you smoking in here. She doesn't like it.

Googin (*chokes, takes cigar from mouth, looks at it*). What kind of a stogie is it, Mr. Williams?

Warren. It's pure Havana. Santas Odoriferous.

Googin (*smells it*). It's odoriferous all right, all right. Begorry, it smells like someone had been burnin' the beans.

Warren. That's the way all pure Havanas smell.

Googin. I think I'll chop 'em up and smoke 'em in me pipe. Much obliged, sor, and merry Christmas to the both of yeez. Tell yer wife that me and Honoria will be right up. (*Exits R.*)

Enter Kitty *from L.*

Kitty. It's all right now. I left an opening. And I sewed on the last pompon. Warren, don't you think we ought to remember the Googins?

Warren. I do remember them. When people have faces like the Googins one never forgets them.

Kitty. He's such a good janitor. Really, I think we ought to make them a little present.

Warren. But I'm busted, Kitty. Those masquerade tickets will take our last cent.

Kitty. We might give the Googins some little thing here. (*Looks around.*) I have it!

Warren. Yes?

Kitty. We'll give them Aunt Minerva's picture.

Warren. Thank goodness. At last we've found a use for Aunt Minerva's picture. Ever since you hung it up there it's haunted me. But the Googins don't want it.

Kitty. I'm sure they will. They're frightfully poor and it would just match their furniture, I'm sure. Henceforth Aunt Minerva shall shed her light in the basement.

Enter Mrs. Googin *from R., followed by* Googin, *smoking a cigar.*

Mrs. Googin. A merry Christmas to the both of yeez. (*To* Kitty.) Me man Maginnis tould me ye wanted to see me.

Kitty (*at R.*). Yes, indeed; come right in.

Mrs. Googin. I know what it is, darlin'. Sure it's a bit of a prisint fer me and the childer, now ain't it, Mrs. Williams? (*Smiles.*)

Kitty (*at R.*). What a good guesser you are.

Mrs. Googin. The Widow O'Toole, her in Apartment C, was after givin' me one of her ould worn-out waists. But I took her down a peg as quick as a wink. I'm a lady, I am, and me mother was a lady before me, and I don't accept cast-off clothes fer Christmas prisints.

Kitty. You don't. (*At R.C. near front with* Mrs. Googin.)

Googin (*at rear L. with* Warren). And nather do I.

Mrs. Googin. The ould bachelor in Apartment F gave me a fine prisint. I brung it up to show yeez. (*Shows fancy waste basket, tied with ribbon bows.*) It's a new bunnet. (*Puts it on her head.*) Sure, that's a Christmas prisint that touches me heart.

Kitty. I'm going to give you that picture. (*Points to crayon portrait.*)

Mrs. Googin. The picture of the ould lady, is it?

Kitty. Yes. It's a lovely frame.

Mrs. Googin. And it's a nice lookin' ould lady, too. She looks a little like me own mother, who before she was married to a Mulvaney was a McShane.

Kitty. Warren, take it down.

Warren. With pleasure. (*Takes picture down.*)

Mrs. Googin (*taking the picture*). Sure, I have no picture of me own mother at all, at all. More's the pity. I'll jist take this picture and then I'll be after tellin' all me frinds that it is a likeness of me mother who was a McShane from County Kilkenny. (*Sits R.*)

Googin. Would ye decave yer frinds, Honoria?

Mrs. Googin. A little deception is the spice of life. And besides it looks enough like herself to be her own photygraft. Don't it, Maginnis?

Googin. Sure it looks like a chromo to me.

Mrs. Googin (*angrily*). A chromo, is it?

Googin. Yis, or wan of them comic valentines.

Mrs. Googin. Listen to that now. He says me own mother looks like a chromo and a comic valentine. I'm a lady, I am, and me mother was a lady before me, and if I wasn't a lady, sure I'd break the picture over yer head, Maginnis Googin. Insulted am I and right before me face! (*Weeps.*) Oh, wurra, wurra, that me own ould mother, who was a McShane, should live to see that day whin her daughter's own husband would call her a comic valentine. (*Weeps and rocks back and forth.*)

Googin (*close to her*). I said nawthin' about yer mother, Honoria Googin. I only remarked that the picture resimbled a comic valentine. And it do. And I'll lave it to Mr. Williams whither I'm right or no.

Mrs. Googin (*rises with dignity, goes to* Kitty). I thank ye kindly fer yer prisint, Mrs. Williams, and I wish yeez all the compliments of the season. (*Turns to* Googin *savagely.*) As fer you, Maginnis Googin, ather ye beg me mother's pardon fer yer insults, or it's nather bite ner sup ye'll git in my house this night. (*Sails out at R. carrying picture and waste basket.*)

Googin. Wait a minute. Listen to me, Nora, darlin'. Let me explain. (*Follows her out at R.*)

Warren. Well, there goes Aunt Minerva.

Kitty. And she sent it to us last Christmas.

Warren. I'm glad she decided not to visit us this year. Money is scarce at the end of the month and she's better off in Kankakee. New York isn't any place for Aunt Minerva on Christmas Day.

Kitty. I'm afraid auntie's gait is not quite up to New York in the holiday season.

Warren. I think I'll try on my costume. Are you sure I can get into the ruff now?

Kitty. Oh, yes. Wasn't that stupid of me? Just like making a skirt and then sewing up the top of it. (*Exit* Warren *at L.*)

Enter Googin *from R.*

Googin. Sure, it's a sad time we're havin' down in the basement.

Kitty. What has happened?

Googin. Herself has locked the door of the apartment and divil a bit will she open it at all.

Kitty. Why, Mr. Googin!

Googin. I'm in a pretty pickle now. All me money is locked up in me house with Honoria. You could be doin' me a great favor, if ye would, Mrs. Williams, mum.

Kitty. What is it, Mr. Googin?

Googin. Go down to the basement and tell me wife to open the door to her lawful wedded husband.

Kitty. Why, of course I will. (*Exits R.*)

Googin (*sits down comfortably and lights a cigar from his box*). Sure, it's a sad Christmas for me, so it is, whin Honoria lets an ould picture come bechune a man and his wife. (*Smokes.*) Begorry, I smell something. (*Sniffs.*) It's awful. (*Rises.*) Some wan is burning some rubber. Maybe I've got too much hate on in the radiators. (*Sniffs.*) My, my, what an awful smell. (*Removes cigar and looks at it, smells it, makes horrible grimace.*) Oh, ho, so it's you, is it? (*Throws it in cuspidor.*) No wonder they call it Santas Odoriferous. If that cigar came from Havana they'd ought to take it back there again and give it a dacent burial.

Enter Eddie from R. with the hat in box.

Eddie. Say, Mr. Googin!

Googin. What is it, Eddie?

Eddie. Does you want to buy a nice Christmas present for a lady?

Googin. Maybe I do. What is it?

Eddie. A nice hat. Right in de latest style. Jes' come home from de millinery store. Mis' Lacey gib it to me for a Christmas present, and I ain't got no use for it.

Googin. Begorry, that's a good idea. I'll make peace with me wife. Eddie, I'll trade ye a nice box of cigars for the hat.

Eddie. Is 'em some ob Mistah Williamses cigars?

Googin. They are. Santas Odoriferous.

Eddie. Man, man, I wouldn't deprive you ob dem cigars for de world.
Googin. Sure it's no depravity at all, at all.

Eddie. I'll sell you de hat for two dollars cash money.

Googin. Two dollars, is it?

Eddie. Yas, sah, and it's worth 'bout ten dollars. De lady done say it's worth *more'n* ten dollars.

Googin. I'll take it. (*Takes out old wallet, counts out two dollars in small change and gives it to* Eddie.)

Eddie. Yas, sah. Dat's right.

Googin. There's yer two dollars.

Eddie. And dere's yer hat. (*Gives him box.*) Excuse me, boss. I hears de elevator bell. (*Exits R.*)

Googin (*opens box and looks at the hat*). Begorry, I've been robbed. Eddie! Ye thavin' nagur, come here. Niver in all the world would me wife wear an orange hat. She hates orange worse ner pizen.

Enter Kitty *from R.* Googin *has hat in the box.*

Kitty. It's all right, Mr. Googin. I had a long talk with your wife and she's all ready for you.

Googin. Ready for me? With a flatiron belike.

Kitty. No, no. Her face is wreathed in smiles. She's waiting for you with a real Kilkenny welcome.

Googin (*smiles*). Is she now? Sure, Mrs. Williams, mum, it's a grand lady ye are. Excuse me, mum, but this bein' Christmas day, I was wonderin' whether you'd be after accepting a wee bit of a Christmas present from the likes of me?

Kitty. Why, Mr. Googin, how very kind and thoughtful.

Googin (*hands her the box*). It's here, mum. A fine hat it is. Right out of the millinery store.

Kitty. Oh, thank you so much. I'm just crazy to see it. (*Takes it out.*) What! (*Stares at it.*)

Googin. Ain't it a beauty, mum?

Kitty (*recovering*). Oh, yes, indeed, Mr. Googin. But it is a far too expensive present for you to give me. You'd better give it to your wife. Here, I'll wrap it all up again.

Googin. But me wife won't wear orange.

Kitty. Tell her to take off the orange and replace it with a green bow. I'll give her a nice green gauze bow.

Googin (*smiling*). Will ye now?

Kitty. Yes. Take it down to her now. It will please her so much. She'll welcome you with open arms.

Googin. I'll do it. (*Takes box.*) And I'm much obliged for your trouble, mum. (*Exits R.*)

Kitty. Warren!

Warren (*outside L.*). Yes?

Kitty. Are you dressed yet? It's nearly five o'clock.

Warren. Sure.

Enter Warren *from L., wearing white Pierrot costume.*

Kitty. Oh, it's a dream.

Warren. I feel like a fool. Say, Kittens, you'd better get into yours.

Enter Mrs. Googin *from R. with picture.*

Mrs. Googin (*not seeing Warren*). Sure I had to run up to tell yeez that iverything was all right, Mrs. Williams. And it's a darlin' y' are.

Kitty. Oh, I'm so glad.

Mrs. Googin (*seeing Warren*). Howly snakes of Ireland, what's that?

Kitty. That's Warren.

Mrs. Googin. He gave me such a start. I thought it was wan of them circus clowns got loose, mum.

Warren (*gayly*). Wait till you see me with my paint on. (*Runs out L.*)

Mrs. Googin. Me husband has given me his consint and I can hang up the picture in me drawing-room, and he furthermore says that me mother is a quane and the picture is her perfect likeness.

Kitty. Then I'm sure you'll have a very merry Christmas, Mrs. Googin.

Mrs. Googin. I brought you up a little Christmas gift, mum.

Kitty. You did?

Mrs. Googin (*takes out the hat*). Ain't it a beauty?

Kitty. Indeed it is. But really you should keep that for yourself.

Mrs. Googin. Indade I'll not. I says to Maginnis, says I, "She's trated me like a lady, and I'll trate her like a lady also." So, here's yer Christmas prisint and many happy returns of the day.

Kitty. But this is such an expensive present, Mrs. Googin. Really, I—

Mrs. Googin (*loftily*). What's ixpense bechune frinds?

Kitty. I don't think I ought to accept such a lovely gift.

Mrs. Googin. Ye'll be hurtin' me feelings if ye don't. I'm a lady, Mrs. Williams, and me mother was a lady before me, and I have very, very sensitive feelings.

Kitty (*sighs, then takes hat and box*). Very well, Mrs. Googin. Thank you so much.

Mrs. Googin. And now I'll be goin' back to the basement. I hope ye have a pleasant time at yer party, mum.

Kitty. Thank you, Mrs. Googin.

Mrs. Googin. Are you goin' to fix yerself up like a circus clown, too?

Kitty. Oh, no. I'm to be Pierrette.

Mrs. Googin. Pierrette, is it? Well, look out ye don't git pinched. Merry Christmas. (*Exit R.*)

Enter Warren *from L.*

Warren. Kittens, there's a poor beggar woman out on the back steps. Can't you find something for her?

Kitty. No, I haven't a thing. (*Sees hat box.*) Oh, yes, I have! Tell her to come in. (*Exit* Warren *at L.*) Now, I'll be rid of my Christmas hoodoo. (*Puts hat in box.*)

Enter Hard Times Annie *from L., weeping loudly.*

Annie. Oh, oh! On Christmas day! Just to think of it. Oh! (*Wails.*)

Kitty. What is it, my good woman? What's the matter?

Annie. Oh, mum, it's starving I am. A poor lone widow with sivin little children huddled up in the straw in a stable. No fire have we, no coal have we, no food have we. And on Christmas day, too. (*Cries.*) Could ye let me have a little money, mum?

Kitty (*looks in her purse and shows audience that it is empty.*) No, I haven't any money.

Annie. And it's such hard times we're having. With the cost of living so high and me with sivin children. No fire have we, no coal have we, no food have we.

Kitty. I'm so sorry for you.

Annie. Thank ye kindly, mum. And can you help me a little?

Kitty. How would you like a nice winter hat? It's perfectly new and has never been worn. It's red and orange.

Annie. Oh, lady, yer a fallen angel, so yer are, fallen right down from the skies. I'd rather have a nice winter hat than have a bushel of coal.

Kitty. There it is. And merry Christmas.

Annie. Thank you, mum. Has it got flowers on it or feathers?

Kitty. Feathers.

Annie. Oh, thank ye. Yer a fallen angel; indade ye are, mum.

Kitty. You'd better go out this way. (*Points to R.*) I don't want my husband to see what I've given you.

Annie. I know how it is, mum. I've had two of 'em meself. But nather one was a circus clown, mum. I suppose that makes 'em bad-tempered.

Kitty. Yes, I suppose so. Good-bye.

Annie (*crosses to door R.*). Merry Christmas, mum. And bless ye for what ye have done for me this day. Yer a fallen angel, mum; indeed yer are. (*Exits R.*)

Enter Warren *from L.*

Warren. Get rid of her?

Kitty. Yes. Gave her some little things. Now I must hurry and dress. How nice you look. I'll be ready in ten minutes. (*Exit L.*)

(*Ring at bell R.*)

Warren (*opens the door, admitting* Laura). Hello, Lolly.

Laura. Are you all ready?

Warren. Kittens has just started to dress. Did you get the tickets?

Laura. Yes. Here they are. Jim's waiting for me.

Warren (*takes the two tickets*). Thank you.

Laura. I had an awful time getting the places reserved.

Warren. Ten dollars, aren't they?

Laura. Yes.

Warren. Just a minute, till I get the money. Sit down. Kittens has the money. (*Exit L.*)

Laura (*calls after him*). Hurry, please, Warren.

Warren (*outside*). All right.

Laura *crosses to R. and sits. She takes up the fashion magazine and reads a moment. Rises impatiently and walks around the room, showing marked impatience. After a pause* Kitty *enters from L. wearing a kimono.*

Kitty. Laura!

Laura. Yes, dear.

Kitty. That hat I gave you!

Laura. The hat?

Kitty. Yes, the one I gave you for Christmas. Warren had just given it to me as a present, and as it wasn't becoming to me so I gave it to you. Where is it?

Laura. Why?

Kitty. He put ten dollars in it at the millinery shop. It was hidden in the lining. The ten dollars for the tickets.

Laura. Good heavens!

Kitty. So that pays you for the tickets, doesn't it?

Laura. But I gave it away.

Kitty. Why, Laura!

Laura. It wasn't becoming to me, either. I gave it to Eddie.

Kitty (*weakly*). To Eddie?

Laura. Of course I didn't know it had ten dollars hidden in the lining.

Kitty. I didn't think you'd treat my present that way.

Laura. Now, Kittens—

Kitty (*angrily*). Gave it to the negro elevator boy. Well, I like that! That hat cost ten dollars.

Laura. I never could have worn it.

Kitty. But you shouldn't have given it away.

Laura. Warren gave it to you and you gave it away.

Kitty. That's different.

Laura. Shall I explain to Warren?

Kitty. No; for goodness sakes, don't do that! I haven't a cent to my name and I can't explain to Warren. How can I tell him I gave his Christmas present away?

Laura. Send for Eddie and make him give you the ten dollars.

Kitty. Eddie hasn't got it.

Laura. What did he do with it?

Kitty. I don't know. A beggar woman has the hat now. I saw her with it.

Laura. Then she has the ten dollars.

Kitty. Laura, you'll have to trust me until the first of the month.

Laura (*coldly*). Oh, very well. It's of no importance.

Kitty. Now, Laura—

Laura (*crosses to door R.*). In the future I'd advise you to keep your Christmas presents. I must go now. Jim is waiting for me.

Kitty. Lolly—

Laura. We'll probably see you at the dinner. (*Exit R.*)

Kitty (*crying*). I'll never give another present away as long as I live.

Warren (*outside L.*). Hurry, Kittens; it's almost time to go.

Kitty. In a minute. (*Exits L.*)

Enter Eddie *from R., followed by* Miss Minerva. *She carries the hat in her hand.*

Miss M. That will do, boy. Mr. Williams is my nephew. I'll find him.

Eddie. Lawdy, now she's got de hat. (*Exits R.*)

Enter Warren *from L.*

Warren (*to* Miss M.). I beg pardon?

Miss M. Heavens!

Warren. What's the matter?

Miss M. I thought you were a ghost.

Warren. I am Mr. Williams.

Miss M. You are? (Drops everything, runs to him and shakes both his hands heartily.) Don't you know me?

Warren. No; never saw you before in my life.

Miss M. I'm your Aunt Minerva.

Warren. Not Aunt Minerva Mockridge from Kankakee?

Miss M. (*positively*). Aunt Minerva Mockridge from Kankakee.

Warren. But I thought you said you weren't coming.[Pg 224]

Miss M. I changed my mind. And I wanted to surprise you and Kitty.

Warren. Well, you did. You've surprised us all right.

Miss M. Let me sit down. I've had such an adventure. (Holds up hat.) See what I brought you?

Warren. A hat?

Miss M. Yes, what's left of it.

Warren. It looks just like the one I gave Kittens for a Christmas present.

Miss M. I got out of the taxi at the corner and was walking along trying to find the house when all of a sudden I heard a great commotion down the street behind me. I turned around and just then a man darted right at me, slapped the hat in my hand and was off like the wind. A crowd of policemen were chasing him. I slipped into the vestibule of a building and luckily it was this house.

Enter Eddie *and* Hogan *from R.*

Eddie. You can't come in yere. Not unless you got a search warrant.

Hogan. I saw her run into the vestibule, boy—and I'll find her if I have to search every apartment from piano to ice-box. (*Sees* Miss M.) There she is now. That woman just came up in the elevator, didn't she?

Eddie. Yassir, boss; dat's de one.

Hogan (*goes to* Miss M.). Come on with me. I guess I've got you at last.

Miss M. What do you mean?

Warren. Officer, this lady is my aunt. I am Mr. Williams, the owner of this apartment.

Hogan (*to* Eddie). Is that man the owner of this apartment?

Eddie. Yessir, boss; dat's Mr. Williams.

Hogan. And you say this lady is your aunt?

Miss M. Of course I'm his aunt.

Hogan. That'll do you! Keep still or I'll put the bracelets on ye.

Warren. Well, she *said* she was my aunt.

Hogan. Have ye ever seen her before?

Warren. No, sir.

Hogan (*turns to* Eddie *at R.*). Ye hear? He thinks she's his aunt and yet he niver seen her before. This woman is a crook. One of the worst in the country. She's old Boston Bell and is wanted in Omaha for highway robbery, in Salt Lake for arson, in Chicago for shoplifting, in Columbus for assault and battery, and in New York for receiving stolen goods.

Warren. And I thought she was my Aunt Minerva.

Miss M. (*at L.C.*). Warren Williams, are you going to let that man stand there and insult me? Throw him out of your house.

Hogan (*C.*). I was standing on me beat when I saw Dopey Daniel snatch a swell hat from a poor old woman. She screams and he hot-foots it down the street with me after him. This dame was standing at the corner. She was working with him. He saw we had him all right, so he slipped the hat to her and she made a getaway up the elevator. Come on, Boston Bell. I've got you with the goods on you. I want that hat for evidence. Now will you come easy or must I use the cuffs? (*Pulls her to door R.*)

Miss M. (*screams*). Kitty, Kitty! Help, help!

Enter Kitty *from R.*

Kitty. Aunt Minerva! (*Rushes to her and embraces her.*) What is the meaning of all this?

Aunt M. (*at R., weeping*). Oh, Kitty, Kitty, I'm arrested. On my first visit to New York. Oh, why did I ever leave Kankakee?

Kitty. Warren, make him release her.

Hogan. Are you sure she's your aunt?

Kitty. Of course I am. Why, we have her picture. There it is. Oh, no—I'd forgotten.

Hogan. I believe the whole gang of yeez is a bunch of crooks. Yeez look like crooks, all drissed up like clowns and things.

Kitty. Eddie, call the janitor.

Eddie. Here he comes now.

Enter Googin *from R. with* Mrs. Googin.

Hogan. Maginnis Googin, is it yerself?

Googin. What's goin' on here, Hogan. Who's been pinched?

Hogan. This dame is Boston Bell. We got her with the goods. She stole a hat.

Kitty. Why, that's my hat. Isn't it, Warren?

Warren. I thought it looked familiar. (*Takes hat.*) Yes, that's your hat. (*Takes two five-dollar bills from the lining.*) Now, I know it's your hat.

Kitty. But where did you get it, Aunt Minerva?

Miss M. Some man ran into me in the street and left it in my hand.

Googin. Hogan, sure I think you've made a mistake.

Hogan. Do you know these folks, Googin?

Mrs. Googin. I know them, Officer Hogan. It's the Williamses, and they're both perfect ladies. And I'm a lady, and so was me mother before me.

Googin. Hush, Honoria. Ye've been drinkin' too much frozen egg nog.

Mrs. Googin (*crying*). And the ould lady that ye've pinched, sure I blave it's me ould mother from Kilkenny, Ireland. Oh, Maginnis, they've pinched me ould mother.

Googin. It's all a mistake, Hogan.

233

Hogan (*to* Miss M.). Ye say a man ran into you in the street and left this hat in your hand?

Miss M. Yes, sir.

Hogan (*to* Kitty). And you say it's your hat?

Kitty. Of course it is.

Warren (*goes to* Hogan, *gives him a five-dollar bill*). I think that will be all, officer. Merry Christmas.

Hogan. Merry Christmas to all of yeez. (*Exits L., followed by* Eddie.)

Kitty. Mrs. Googin, this is my aunt, Miss Mockridge from Kankakee.

Mrs. Googin. Sure, I thought it was me ould mother from Kilkenny. Ye look enough like her to be her own twin sister, ye do.

Googin. I came up to inform yeez that the taxi do be waiting.

Miss M. Taxi? Are you going out?

Kitty (*looks at* Warren). Well—er—that is—er we—

Warren. Yes, er—we thought you weren't coming.

Miss M. Where are you going?

Kitty. We were going to a masquerade dinner dance, but now that you've come we'll stay at home.

Googin (*to* Miss M.). Ye'd better go to the dance, mum. Ye'll have the time of yer life. Faith, they've nothin' like it in Kankakee. Come on, Honoria.

Mrs. Googin. All of yeez come down and take tea wid me in the marnin' fer breakfast. Merry New Year and happy Christmas to all. I'm a lady and me mother was a lady before me, and I knows a lady whin I sees her. So I wish yeez all a happy Christmas and many of them. (*Exits R. with* Googin.)

Warren. Shall I send the taxi away, Kittens?

Miss M. I should say not. I'm going to that masquerade ball, if it's the last thing I ever do. That's why I came to New York. (*Takes out purse.*) Here's a hundred and twenty dollars. That's enough to see us through until breakfast, isn't it?

Kitty. We mustn't keep the taxi waiting. Come on, auntie. We're going to show you the time of your life.

Miss M. But I haven't any costume.

Kitty (*puts the hat on her head*). There you are. Now you're all fixed. I knew I could make some use of my Christmas hat. Hurry, Warren. (They hurry out R. as curtain falls.)

Curtain.

The End

www.ingramcontent.com/pod-product-compliance
Lightning Source LLC
Chambersburg PA
CBHW070638290526
45790CB00001B/135